THE 99 NAMES GUIDED JOURNAL

LEARN, LOVE & LIVE THE MEANING & BENEFITS OF ALLAH'S NAMES ONE DAY AT A TIME

And to Allah belong the best names, so call upon Him by them ... (Quran 7:180)

Created by Towards Faith

AUDIO REFLECTIONS

As you journey through each name of Allah in this journal, connect with scholars, shuyookh & teachers around the world through their inspirational and thought-provoking audio reflections on Allah's names. Through these audio reflections you can deepen your connection to Allah by understanding His beautiful names with the guidance of our teachers.

ACCESS AUDIO REFLECTIONS AT
WWW.99NAMES.FAITH

HOW TO USE

If you have an Apple device, simply open your camera and scan the QR code above which will take you to our audio reflections website. Bookmark this website for easy access whilst you use the journal.

If you have an Android device, download a QR code reader app and scan the QR code above.

WHO IS YOUR LORD?

For every journey that you take, knowing where and to whom you are travelling to is always the most important step. Think about the experience you go through when you are planning a holiday. What is the first thing that you do? You research the destination. If you are attending an interview for a new job, your first step is to learn more about the company that you have an interview for and to gain an understanding of who will be interviewing you. If you are meeting a new friend or a potential life partner, your first step is to understand who they are, what are their characteristics and attributes, and who they are as a person.

Our ultimate journey in life is towards Allah. Our ultimate destination is to be in paradise with Allah. The ultimate meeting that we all aim to experience is with Allah. But have we spent enough time knowing who Allah is?

When you die, two angels will approach you and they will ask you three questions. Do you know what the first question is? It's "Who is your Lord?" and our answer ultimately decides our final fate.

Our sincerest intention in creating this journal is to help you answer this question.

One of the reasons Allah - exalted is He - has revealed some of His names and attributes is so that we can know Him, making worshiping Him and submitting to Him beloved to us. Think about this: you, as a human being, have multiple attributes and characteristics, but you do not reveal all of them. You reveal what is relevant for the person in front of you to know about you, and what is important for your relationship.

So, what does this mean when Allah reveals and emphasizes that, for example, He is the Most Merciful? What is significant and beautiful about Allah's Names is that through them, we can see how our Creator recognizes our needs, and how deeply He knows us. We all need sustenance; and He is ar-Razzāq, The Provider. We all need love; and He is al-Wadūd, The Most Loving. We all need protection; and Allah is al-Ḥafīẓ, The Guardian. While we can be given a measure of what we need through people (and that is only through Allah's permission), what is with people is naturally limited. Allah, on the other hand, is unlimited.

Thus, sometimes we are put through certain situations to get to know Allah through the manifestation of His different names. Sometimes it is to open our eyes to your own flaws so that we can change. Whatever the lesson is, if we realize that the answer to any problem is through Him, and that He suffices all our needs, then our relief is already at hand. And this can only happen through knowing Him through the names He has revealed to us.

> **" And to Allah belong the best names, so call upon Him by them ...**
> **(7:180)** **"**

The purpose of this journal is to help you to learn, love and live these names so that you can call upon Allah in the times that you need it the most and finally learn who He is.

In a well-known and sound statement by the Prophet Muhammad ﷺ, he informs us that "Allah has ninety-nine names and whoever preserves them will enter Paradise." (Bukhari and Muslim)

There are three important matters to understand in this hadith: the number of Allah's names, what His names are and how we ascertain them, and, finally, the meaning of "preserves them".

In regards to the first issue, the hadith does not limit Allah's names to 99, as some people might assume. Rather, Allah has more than 99 names, but if we understand and live by at least 99 of them, then Allah will grant us Paradise. The fact that Allah has more than 99 names is alluded to in the following supplication by our beloved Prophet ﷺ:

"O Allah, I am your servant, the son of your servant, the son of your maidservant. My forelock is in your hand, your command concerning me prevails, and your decision concerning me is just. I call upon you by every one of the beautiful names with which you have described yourself, or which you have revealed in your Book, or you have taught to any of your creatures, or which you have chosen to keep in the knowledge of the unseen with you, to make the Qur'an the delight of my soul, the light of my heart, and to remove my sadness and dispel my anxiety."
(Aḥmad)

HOW TO USE

01 — TAKE ONE STEP AT A TIME

Take one name at a time, internalise and reflect on that name until you are comfortable with what it means and you can relate to it. Use the audio reflections, knowledge and journaling space for an all-encompassing experience that allows you to deepen your understanding and relationship with Allah.

02 — DON'T SHELF IT

If you place this on a shelf that you don't interact with then most likely you will never learn and internalise the names. Place it somewhere clean and accessible such as your daily desk or bedside table. Set aside a time in the day where you can go through a name of Allah and reflect on it.

SUPPLICATIONS

We have included some examples of supplications you could make as a prompt. However, the most powerful supplication is one that comes from the heart. Understand His names, reflect upon them, and then call upon Allah with His names in a way that you feel connected to.

SITUATIONS SUPPORT

To call upon Him using His names is the ultimate goal of this journal. We've created a situations index where we've matched up typical life situations you may go through to the names of Allah you can call upon for each situation. These are simply suggestions to help you to turn to Him through the various situations you find yourself in, but you are encouraged contemplate over your own personal relationship with each of the names.

SITUATIONS SUPPORT

ANXIOUS & OVERWHELMED	As-Salām, Aṣ-Ṣamad, Al-'Azīz, Al-Kabīr, Al-Muhaymin, Al-Qawī
ARROGANT	Al-Quddūs, Al-'Alī, Al-Muta'āl, Al-'Azīm, Al-Khāfiḍ, Ar-Rāfi', Al-Mutakabbir, Al-Mu'izz, Al-Mudhill, Al-'Azīz
ASPIRED	Al-'Alī, Al-Muta'āl, Al-Wārith
DISTANT FROM ALLAH	Al-Mujīb, Al-Ḥalīm, At-Tawwāb, Al-Awwal, Al-Ākhir, Al-Mubdi', Al-Mu'īd, Al-Khāliq
DISTANT FROM OTHERS	Al-Jāmi'
EMPTY	Aẓ-Ẓāhir, Al-Bāṭin
GUILTY OF SIN	Al-Ghafūr, Al-Ghaffār, Al-'Afuww
HAPPY	Al-Wahhāb
IMPATIENT	Aṣ-Ṣabūr
INCAPABLE	Al-Wāsi'
INJUSTICE	Al-'Adl, Al-Malik, Mālik al-Mulk, Al-Qahhār, Ash-Shahīd, Al-Muntaqim, Al-'Azīz
JEALOUS	Al-Khāfiḍ, Ar-Rāfi'
JUDGING OTHERS	Al-Bāri'
WEAK	Al-Mu'min, Al-Badī', Al-Qawī

Al-Wakīl, Al-Ghanī, Al-Mughnī, Al-Wāhid, Al-Ahad, Al-Hasīb, Al-Muqīt, Al-Hasīb	LET DOWN BY OTHERS
Al-Walī, Al-Walī,	LONELY
Ar-Rashīd, Al-Muhaymin, Al-Fattāh, Al-Qābid, Al-Bāsit, An-Nūr, Al-Haqq, Al-Matīn, Al-Hādī, Al-Qādir, Al-Qadīr, Al-Muqtadir, Al-Muhaymin, Al-Hasīb	LOST
Al-Musawwir, Al-'Azīz	LOW SELF-CONFIDENCE
Al-Jalīl, Dhū al-Jalāl wa al-Ikrām, Al-Bā'ith, Al-Wārith, Al-Malik, Mālik al-Mulk, Al-Majīd, Al-Mājid, Al-Wāhid, Al-Ahad	MATERIALISTIC
Ar-Rahmān, Ar-Rahīm	MERCILESS
Al-Muhsī, Al-'Alīm, Al-Samī'	MISUNDERSTOOD
Al-Muqīt	SPIRITUALLY LOW
Al-Basīr, Ar-Raqīb, Al-Bāqī, Al-Muhsī, Al-Qahhār, Al-Hādī	TEMPTATION & SIN
Al-Barr, Ar-Ra'ūf	UNKIND
Ash-Shakūr, Al-Karīm	UNGRATEFUL
Al-Muqsit	UNJUST
Al-Hafīz	UNPROTECTED
Al-Jalīl, Dhū al-Jalāl wa al-Ikrām, Al-Latīf, Al-Razzāq, Al-Hayy, Al-Wājid, Al-Māni', Al-Muhaymin, As-Samad	UNSUPPORTED
Al-Hamīd, Al-Hakīm, Al-Hakam	UPSET AT THE OUTCOME

THE 99 NAMES GUIDED JOURNAL

LEARN, LOVE & LIVE THE MEANING & BENEFITS OF ALLAH'S NAMES ONE DAY AT A TIME

الرَّحْمٰـنِ الرَّحِيمِ

AR-RAHMĀN
AR-RAHĪM

THE ENTIRELY MERCIFUL, THE ESPECIALLY MERCIFUL

'In the name of Allah, the Entirely Merciful, the Especially Merciful' (1:1)

STORY

How do you introduce yourself, aside from saying your name? You likely mention different things depending on the situation and your relationship with the other person. If you could only say a few things, you would mention the most important thing that you want the other person to know. What would it be for you? Allah is far above any analogy, but when He introduces Himself to us, out of all of the names He could have chosen, He introduces Himself in the opening chapter of the Quran as the 'Entirely Merciful, the Especially Merciful' (1:1), and we start the recitation of the Qur'an with these names. To further emphasize this, He tells us that His name ar-Raḥmān is interchangeable with His name Allah (17:110). Therefore what defines our relationship with our Creator is mercy. His mercy towards all His creation is manifested in the everyday blessings and comforts around us that we may overlook, such as the night and day, random kindness from those around us, or relief that comes after distress. His specific mercy for the believers is manifested in, for example, Ramadan, when they are given an increase in blessings and reward. Prayer in the last third of the night is an intimate time between one and God, and there is a special bond between one who wakes up at this time to connect to ar-Raḥīm. From His mercy is that in the Hereafter, one dip in Paradise for the person who faced the most hardships in this world will erase any former feeling of distress or pain. While His name ar-Raḥmān is unique to Him, He describes His Prophet as Raḥīm and the believers as having mercy for one another. Thus, a believer tries to exhibit and embody mercy in all his or her interactions.

Ar-Raḥmān is the One who is the All Merciful and the Entirely Merciful, with His mercy being immediate and all-encompassing, embracing everything He has created. Ar-Raḥīm is the Especially Merciful and the Ever-Merciful, who has the permanent attribute of mercy, and a special kind for His believing servants.

- At-Tawwāb - The Relenting (2:54)
- Al-Ghafūr - The Oft-Forgiving (6:54)
- Ar-Ra'ūf - The Pitying (57:9)
- Al-Azīz - The Almighty (26:9)
- Al-Barr - The Kind (52:28)

- If ever we are tempted to treat others harshly, we should remember that Allah's mercy encompasses them, so should we not extend to them compassion?

Ya Raḥmān Ya Raḥīm, let us never despair of Your mercy, guide us to be merciful to others.

How can you introduce the characteristic of being merciful to others in your life and how would that make you feel?

المَلِك، مالك المُلك

AL-MALIK
MĀLIK AL-MULK
THE KING, THE POSSESSOR OF SOVEREIGNTY

'He is Allah, other than whom there is no deity, the King, the Pure...' (59:23)

STORY

The idea of a king may inspire awe and reverence in people because a king by definition has power and authority over his kingdom. Yet, it may also arouse feelings of fear or contempt when one thinks of human kings, who may use their power and position to perpetuate injustice or for personal gain. Allah is the true King and Possessor of everything in His kingdom, and His names and attributes are free from the defects of mortal manifestations. This means that Allah has ultimate power and authority over His creation, but it is exercised with wisdom and justice as is befitting His majesty. This name reminds us that we all live in the 'kingdom' of al-Malik, Mālik al-Mulk, and therefore, we need to live by His rules. While we should take comfort in knowing His mercy, we must be vigilant over our misdeeds because we will all be brought before the King on the Day of Judgment. Imagine standing before Allah, al-Malik - what would you be feeling? A true King is both generous and just, so we have hope that al-Malik will give us from His bounty, and overlook our slip-ups. At the same time, if we oppress others, we should know that al-Malik - the True King - would never accept that, and will hold all oppressors to account. This should inspire us to hold ourselves to account before we are held to account. We need to always remind ourselves that we are living on Allah's earth, and everything we have is ultimately His, and this should redefine our relationship with the things around us.

Al-Malik is the One who is the Ultimate Sovereign and King, and Mālik al-Mulk is the One who is the True Possessor of everything that exists.

- Al-Ḥaqq - The Truth (23:116)
- Al-Quddūs - The Pure (59:23)

- When you feel overwhelmed by the injustices in the world.
- When you become attached to your possessions.

Ya Malik, Ya Mālik al-Mulk guide us in being just in all our daily affairs, our possessions and our relationships.

What is one thing you can do everyday to recognise that you are living in the kingdom of al-Malik, Mālik al-Mulk?

MEMORIZATION LIST

Ar-Raḥmān	1
Ar-Raḥīm	2
Al-Malik	3
Al-Quddūs	**4**
As-Salām	5
Al-Mu'min	6
Al-Muhaymin	7
Al-'Azīz	8
Al-Jabbār	9
Al-Mutakabbir	10
Al-Khāliq	11
Al-Bāri'	12
Al-Muṣawwir	13
Al-Ghaffār	14
Al-Qahhār	15
Al-Wahhāb	16
Ar-Razzāq	17
Al-Fattāḥ	18
Al-'Alīm	19
Al-Qābiḍ	20
Al-Bāsiṭ	21
Al-Khāfiḍ	22
Ar-Rāfi'	23
Al-Muizz	24
Al-Mudhill	25
As-Samī'	26
Al-Baṣīr	27
Al-Ḥakam	28
Al-'Adl	29
Al-Laṭīf	30
Al-Khabīr	31
Al-Ḥalīm	32
Al-'Aẓīm	33
Al-Ghafūr	34
Ash-Shakūr	35
Al-'Alī	36
Al-Kabīr	37
Al-Ḥafīẓ	38
Al-Muqīt	39
Al-Ḥasīb	40
Al-Jalīl	41
Al-Karīm	42
Ar-Raqīb	43
Al-Mujīb	44
Al-Wāsi'	45
Al-Ḥakīm	46
Al-Wadūd	47
Al-Majīd	48
Al-Bā'ith	49
Ash-Shahīd	50
Al-Ḥaqq	51
Al-Wakīl	52
Al-Qawī	53
Al-Matīn	54
Al-Walī	55
Al-Ḥamīd	56
Al-Muḥṣī	57
Al-Mubdi'	58
Al-Mu'īd	59
Al-Muḥyī	60
Al-Mumīt	61
Al-Ḥayy	62
Al-Qayyūm	63
Al-Wājid	64
Al-Mājid	65
Al-Wāḥid	66
Al-Aḥad	67
Aṣ-Ṣamad	68
Al-Qādir	69
Al-Qadīr	70
Al-Muqtadir	71
Al-Muqaddim	72
Al-Mu'akhir	73
Al-Awwal	74
Al-Ākhir	75
Aẓ-Ẓāhir	76
Al-Bāṭin	77
Al-Wālī	78
Al-Muta'āl	79
Al-Barr	80
At-Tawwāb	81
Al-Muntaqim	82
Al-'Afuww	83
Ar-Ra'ūf	84
Mālik al-Mulk	85
Dhū al-Jalāl wa al-Ikrām	86
Al-Muqsiṭ	87
Al-Jāmi'	88
Al-Ghanī	89
Al-Mughnī	90
Al-Māni'	91
Aḍ-Ḍārr	92
An-Nāfi'	93
An-Nūr	94
Al-Hādī	95
Al-Badī'	96
Al-Bāqī	97
Al-Wārith	98
Ar-Rashīd	99
Aṣ-Ṣabūr	100
Allāh	101

TRACE

الْقُدُّوس

AL-QUDDŪS

THE PURE

'He is Allah , other than whom there is no deity, the Sovereign, the Pure...' **(59:23)**

STORY

Different religions and cultures conceptualize God or a Divine entity in different ways. What runs through many understandings, however, is the tendency to anthropomorphize God - to give Him human qualities. But the Qur'an makes clear, 'Nothing is like Him.' (42:11). The name al-Quddūs alerts us to this: whenever we attach to Allah human qualities - a short temper, an inability to forgive, haste, desires and passions - these human iterations of whatever attribute we think of are negated by Him being al-Quddūs. Allah is the Pure and the Holy, and He is therefore purified from anything blameworthy. It means that His attributes are far beyond human conception because we have never witnessed anything like them in human form. So if we doubt that Allah's mercy will encompass us, perhaps because we have never seen complete mercy from other people, we need to remind ourselves: He is al-Quddūs, and that means that His mercy is far above what we can conceive. When we wonder how justice will be served, because the justice systems in this world are flawed, we remember: al-Quddūs is the one who will deliver true, pure justice.

He is purified from any defect or flaw, and all of His names and attributes are also pure and free from imperfection. Every name is in its purest, highest form, with no deficiency.

- Al-Malik - The Sovereign (59:23, Bukhari)
- Al-Subbūḥ - Exhalted (Muslim)

- When you find yourself wondering about how God manifests His name and attributes, and what His mercy or His justice look like, remember that they are the most perfect forms of mercy and justice.

Ya Quddūs, you are the Pure One. Lead us to a sound belief in Your oneness, help us in purifying our hearts, deeds, and intentions.

Do you sanctify what Allah has sanctified? Do you respect what He has told us is holy?

MEMORIZATION LIST

Ar-Rahmān — 1 ○
Ar-Rahīm — 2 ○
Al-Malik — 3 ○
Al-Quddūs — 4 ○
As-Salām — 5 ○
Al-Mu'min — 6 ○
Al-Muhaymin — 7 ○
Al-'Azīz — 8 ○
Al-Jabbār — 9 ○
Al-Mutakabbir — 10 ○
Al-Khāliq — 11 ○
Al-Bāri' — 12 ○
Al-Muṣawwir — 13 ○
Al-Ghaffār — 14 ○
Al-Qahhār — 15 ○
Al-Wahhāb — 16 ○
Ar-Razzāq — 17 ○
Al-Fattāḥ — 18 ○
Al-'Alīm — 19 ○
Al-Qābiḍ — 20 ○
Al-Bāsiṭ — 21 ○
Al-Khāfiḍ — 22 ○
Ar-Rāfi' — 23 ○
Al-Mu'izz — 24 ○
Al-Mudhill — 25 ○
As-Samī' — 26 ○
Al-Baṣīr — 27 ○
Al-Hakam — 28 ○
Al-'Adl — 29 ○
Al-Laṭīf — 30 ○
Al-Khabīr — 31 ○
Al-Halīm — 32 ○
Al-'Aẓīm — 33 ○
Al-Ghafūr — 34 ○
Ash-Shakūr — 35 ○
Al-'Alī — 36 ○
Al-Kabīr — 37 ○
Al-Hafīz — 38 ○
Al-Muqīt — 39 ○
Al-Hasīb — 40 ○
Al-Jalīl — 41 ○
Al-Karīm — 42 ○
Ar-Raqīb — 43 ○
Al-Mujīb — 44 ○
Al-Wāsi' — 45 ○
Al-Hakīm — 46 ○
Al-Wadūd — 47 ○
Al-Majīd — 48 ○
Al-Bā'ith — 49 ○
Ash-Shahīd — 50 ○
Al-Haqq — 51 ○
Al-Wakīl — 52 ○
Al-Qawī — 53 ○
Al-Matīn — 54 ○
Al-Walī — 55 ○
Al-Hamīd — 56 ○
Al-Muhṣī — 57 ○
Al-Mubdi' — 58 ○
Al-Mu'īd — 59 ○
Al-Muhyī — 60 ○
Al-Mumīt — 61 ○
Al-Hayy — 62 ○
Al-Qayyūm — 63 ○
Al-Wājid — 64 ○
Al-Mājid — 65 ○
Al-Wāhid — 66 ○
Al-Ahad — 67 ○
As-Ṣamad — 68 ○
Al-Qādir — 69 ○
Al-Qadīr — 70 ○
Al-Muqtadir — 71 ○
Al-Muqaddim — 72 ○
Al-Mu'akhir — 73 ○
Al-Awwal — 74 ○
Al-Ākhir — 75 ○
Az-Zāhir — 76 ○
Al-Bāṭin — 77 ○
Al-Wālī — 78 ○
Al-Muta'ālī — 79 ○
Al-Barr — 80 ○
At-Tawwāb — 81 ○
Al-Muntaqim — 82 ○
Al-'Afuww — 83 ○
Ar-Ra'ūf — 84 ○
Mālik al-Mulk — 85 ○
Dhū al-Jalāl wa al-Ikrām — 86 ○
Al-Muqsiṭ — 87 ○
Al-Jāmi' — 88 ○
Al-Ghanī — 89 ○
Al-Mughnī — 90 ○
Al-Māni' — 91 ○
Ad-Dārr — 92 ○
An-Nāfi' — 93 ○
An-Nūr — 94 ○
Al-Hādī — 95 ○
Al-Badī' — 96 ○
Al-Bāqī — 97 ○
Al-Wārith — 98 ○
Ar-Rashīd — 99 ○
As-Ṣabūr — 100 ○
Allāh — 101 ○

AS-SALĀM

THE SOURCE OF PEACE AND PERFECTION

'He is Allah, other than whom there is no deity,
the Sovereign, the Pure, the Peace...' (59:23)

STORY

Perhaps what unites all human beings is our search for peace. We do this in different ways: the necessary things, such as working in order to have peace from poverty or need, beneficial practices such as meditation to 'switch off', and perhaps we even engage in unhealthy activities to fill the lack of peace in our hearts. As-Salām teaches us where to look: true peace can only be found with Him. This is why we say after every prayer: 'O Allah, You are Peace and from You is peace. Blessed are You, the Majestic and the Noble.' (Muslim). We remind ourselves that true peace can only be found with Him and in what He has prescribed as a healing for our soul. Moreover, we can feel the manifestations of as-Salām in moments of serenity. Witnessing the beauty of the natural world, and the feelings of tranquility that come with that, are part of that manifestation. Internal calm in the face of hardships is from the Giver of Peace. The sound or secure heart is one that is cleared of spiritual diseases, such as envy and rancor, and is filled with as-Salām instead. This requires active purification. Peace is both an internal and external state. When the Prophet ﷺ arrived in Madina, he made the famous statement, 'O people, spread peace, feed the hungry, and pray at night when people are sleeping and you will enter Paradise in peace.' (Tirmidhī) Outwardly, being a servant of as-Salām means, at the very least, not harming others. At a higher level, it is actively spreading Allah's peace through cordial relations, preventing harm, and teaching about the ways to Peace.

MEANING

The Flawless One who is free from fault or defect, who is both the Source and Giver of peace.

PAIRING

- Al-Quddūs - The Pure (59:23)
- Al-Mu'min - The Granter of Security (59:23)

SITUATION

- When you feel combative, anxiety or stress, seek calm from Him.
- When you greet other people (as-salamu 'alaykum — Peace be upon you), remember that you are guaranteeing them peace from you and praying for peace for them from as-Salām.

DU'A

Ya Salām, guide us to patience and inner peace, and let us remember you more so that we may find peace.

REFLECTIVE QUESTION

When do you suffer from anxiety or stressful situations and how can you cultivate a practice of remembering as-Salām during those times?

الْمُؤْمِنُ

AL-MU'MIN

THE GRANTER OF SECURITY

'He is God: there is no god other than Him, the Controller, the Holy One, Source of Peace, Granter of Security.' (59:23)

STORY

As human beings, there might be multiple things that we fear. We may have small quirks such as a fear of insects or a larger fear over our sustenance or harm from others. Knowing al-Mu'min is knowing that true security is found with Him, and that He secures His righteous servants. Indeed, when the mother of Moses (as) felt emptiness and fear after placing her child in the river, God tells us that He 'strengthened it [her heart] to make her one of those who believe [al-mu'minīn].' [28:10] Our understanding of security must go beyond physical security. The ultimate security is the security of faith we are bestowed with, and this gives us the strength to withstand the hardships of life. He also grants us security through the truth of His revelation, meaning that we do not have to keep guessing as to what Allah wants from us or be worried that He might break His promise. Part of His security is that He ensures that you can trust in His words completely.

MEANING

The One who grants security, be that physical security, emotional security, or spiritual security for those who believe in Him.

PAIRING

- As-Salām - The Source of Peace (59:23)
- Al-Muhaymin - The Overseeing Guardian (59:23)

SITUATION

- When you feel fear, or weak in faith.
- When you think of your role as a mu'min i.e. as a believer, give other people security from yourself by being truthful.

DU'A

Ya Mu'min, bless us with strong eman, allow us to seek security from You and give others security from ourselves.

REFLECTIVE QUESTION

What do you feel insecure about in your life and how might you now make du'a to Allah using His name al-Mu'min to help you overcome those insecurities?

MEMORIZATION LIST

Ar-Raḥmān — 1 ○
Ar-Raḥīm — 2 ○
Al-Malik — 3 ○
Al-Quddūs — 4 ○
As-Salām — 5 ○
Al-Mu'min — 6 ○
Al-Muhaymin — 7 ○
Al-'Azīz — 8 ○
Al-Jabbār — 9 ○
Al-Mutakabbir — 10 ○
Al-Khāliq — 11 ○
Al-Bāri' — 12 ○
Al-Muṣawwir — 13 ○
Al-Ghaffār — 14 ○
Al-Qahhār — 15 ○
Al-Wahhāb — 16 ○
Ar-Razzāq — 17 ○
Al-Fattāḥ — 18 ○
Al-'Alīm — 19 ○
Al-Qābid — 20 ○
Al-Bāsit — 21 ○
Al-Khāfiḍ — 22 ○
Ar-Rāfi' — 23 ○
Al-Muizz — 24 ○
Al-Mudhill — 25 ○
As-Samī' — 26 ○
Al-Baṣīr — 27 ○
Al-Hakam — 28 ○
Al-'Adl — 29 ○
Al-Laṭīf — 30 ○
Al-Khabīr — 31 ○
Al-Ḥalīm — 32 ○
Al-'Azīm — 33 ○
Al-Ghafūr — 34 ○
Ash-Shakūr — 35 ○
Al-'Alī — 36 ○
Al-Kabīr — 37 ○
Al-Ḥafīz — 38 ○
Al-Muqīt — 39 ○
Al-Ḥasīb — 40 ○
Al-Jalīl — 41 ○
Al-Karīm — 42 ○
Ar-Raqīb — 43 ○
Al-Mujīb — 44 ○
Al-Wāsi' — 45 ○
Al-Ḥakīm — 46 ○
Al-Wadūd — 47 ○
Al-Majīd — 48 ○
Al-Bā'ith — 49 ○
Ash-Shahīd — 50 ○
Al-Ḥaqq — 51 ○
Al-Wakīl — 52 ○
Al-Qawī — 53 ○
Al-Matīn — 54 ○
Al-Walī — 55 ○
Al-Ḥamīd — 56 ○
Al-Muḥṣī — 57 ○
Al-Mubdi' — 58 ○
Al-Mu'īd — 59 ○
Al-Muḥyī — 60 ○
Al-Mumīt — 61 ○
Al-Ḥayy — 62 ○
Al-Qayyūm — 63 ○
Al-Wājid — 64 ○
Al-Majid — 65 ○
Al-Wāḥid — 66 ○
Al-Aḥad — 67 ○
Aṣ-Ṣamad — 68 ○
Al-Qādir — 69 ○
Al-Qadīr — 70 ○
Al-Muqtadir — 71 ○
Al-Muqaddim — 72 ○
Al-Mu'akhir — 73 ○
Al-Awwal — 74 ○
Al-Ākhir — 75 ○
Az-Zāhir — 76 ○
Al-Bāṭin — 77 ○
Al-Walī — 78 ○
Al-Muta'āl — 79 ○
Al-Barr — 80 ○
At-Tawwāb — 81 ○
Al-Muntaqim — 82 ○
Al-'Afuww — 83 ○
Ar-Ra'ūf — 84 ○
Mālik al-Mulk — 85 ○
Dhū al-Jalāl wa al-Ikrām — 86 ○
Al-Muqsiṭ — 87 ○
Al-Jāmi' — 88 ○
Al-Ghanī — 89 ○
Al-Mughnī — 90 ○
Al-Māni' — 91 ○
Aḍ-Ḍārr — 92 ○
An-Nāfi' — 93 ○
An-Nūr — 94 ○
Al-Hādī — 95 ○
Al-Badī' — 96 ○
Al-Bāqī — 97 ○
Al-Wārith — 98 ○
Ar-Rashīd — 99 ○
Aṣ-Ṣabūr — 100 ○
Allāh — 101 ○

المُهَيْمِن

AL-MUHAYMIN

THE OVERSEEING GUARDIAN

'He is God: there is no god other than Him, the Controller, the Holy One, Source of Peace, Granter of Security, Guardian over all...' (59:23)

STORY

Generally, when one is described as having haymanah, it means that they oversee what is under their control and they guard it. If you were worried that you were in trouble, whether at work, at home, or at school, your peer reassuring you would not really put you at ease. Even one who is your senior would not reassure you, at least not completely, because they are not the ones in control. You would, however, be put at ease when the one who is truly in control gives you instruction, or tells you that you are ok. God is far above any analogy, but it is He who oversees, controls, and guards completely and perfectly. Thus, we can seek comfort in knowing that despite what others might believe that they have of control, they do not and, as long as we are on the right path, God is muhaymin over our affairs. We can turn straight to the Qur'an and the sunnah of the Messenger to know what the One who is truly in control has said is the best way for us to follow.

MEANING

The One who oversees all, is in control of everything, and is the perfect guardian.

PAIRING

- Al-Mu'min -The Granter of Security (59:23)
- Al-'Aziz - the Almighty (59:23)

SITUATION

- When things in your life feel out of control, for example at work.
- When others exert control over you that is unjust.

DU'A

Ya Muhaymin please do not leave us in charge of our affairs, you are the guardian and controller, allow us to be content with your decree.

REFLECTIVE QUESTION

When do you feel out of control in your life? How might you begin to remember Al-Muhaymin during these times to give you comfort?

MEMORIZATION LIST

Ar-Raḥmān	1 ○
Ar-Raḥīm	2 ○
Al-Malik	3 ○
Al-Quddūs	4 ○
As-Salām	5 ○
Al-Mu'min	6 ○
Al-Muhaymin	7 ○
Al-'Azīz	**8 ○**
Al-Jabbār	9 ○
Al-Mutakabbir	10 ○
Al-Khāliq	11 ○
Al-Bāri'	12 ○
Al-Muṣawwir	13 ○
Al-Ghaffār	14 ○
Al-Qahhār	15 ○
Al-Wahhāb	16 ○
Ar-Razzāq	17 ○
Al-Fattāḥ	18 ○
Al-'Alīm	19 ○
Al-Qābiḍ	20 ○
Al-Bāsiṭ	21 ○
Al-Khāfiḍ	22 ○
Ar-Rāfi'	23 ○
Al-Muizz	24 ○
Al-Mudhill	25 ○
As-Samī'	26 ○
Al-Baṣīr	27 ○
Al-Ḥakam	28 ○
Al-'Adl	29 ○
Al-Laṭīf	30 ○
Al-Khabīr	31 ○
Al-Ḥalīm	32 ○
Al-'Aẓīm	33 ○
Al-Ghafūr	34 ○
Ash-Shakūr	35 ○
Al-'Alī	36 ○
Al-Kabīr	37 ○
Al-Ḥafīẓ	38 ○
Al-Muqīt	39 ○
Al-Ḥasīb	40 ○
Al-Jalīl	41 ○
Al-Karīm	42 ○
Ar-Raqīb	43 ○
Al-Mujīb	44 ○
Al-Wāsi'	45 ○
Al-Ḥakīm	46 ○
Al-Wadūd	47 ○
Al-Majīd	48 ○
Al-Bā'ith	49 ○
Ash-Shahīd	50 ○
Al-Ḥaqq	51 ○
Al-Wakīl	52 ○
Al-Qawī	53 ○
Al-Matīn	54 ○
Al-Walī	55 ○
Al-Ḥamīd	56 ○
Al-Muḥṣī	57 ○
Al-Mubdi'	58 ○
Al-Mu'īd	59 ○
Al-Muḥyī	60 ○
Al-Mumīt	61 ○
Al-Ḥayy	62 ○
Al-Qayyūm	63 ○
Al-Wājid	64 ○
Al-Mājid	65 ○
Al-Wāhid	66 ○
Al-Aḥad	67 ○
Aṣ-Ṣamad	68 ○
Al-Qādir	69 ○
Al-Qadīr	70 ○
Al-Muqtadir	71 ○
Al-Muqaddim	72 ○
Al-Mu'akhir	73 ○
Al-Awwal	74 ○
Al-Ākhir	75 ○
Az-Ẓāhir	76 ○
Al-Bāṭin	77 ○
Al-Walī	78 ○
Al-Muta'āl	79 ○
Al-Barr	80 ○
At-Tawwāb	81 ○
Al-Muntaqim	82 ○
Al-'Afuww	83 ○
Ar-Ra'ūf	84 ○
Mālik al-Mulk	85 ○
Dhū al-Jalāl wa al-Ikrām	86 ○
Al-Muqsiṭ	87 ○
Al-Jāmi'	88 ○
Al-Ghanī	89 ○
Al-Mughnī	90 ○
Al-Māni'	91 ○
Aḍ-Ḍārr	92 ○
An-Nāfi'	93 ○
An-Nūr	94 ○
Al-Hādī	95 ○
Al-Badī'	96 ○
Al-Bāqī	97 ○
Al-Wārith	98 ○
Ar-Rashīd	99 ○
Aṣ-Ṣabūr	100 ○
Allāh	101 ○

AL-'AZĪZ

THE ALMIGHTY

'Whoever desires honor - then to Allah belongs all honor [al-izza].' (35:10)

STORY

We are given numerous examples in the Qur'an of those who appear to be weak, but they were strengthened by God due to their righteousness and faith in Him. If one were to ask, 'who was stronger, Āsiyah (the wife of Pharaoh) or Pharaoh?' The answer should be clear: While she was physically and socially weaker, al-'Azīz granted her honor and strength - 'izzah. Āsiyah was able to stand up to a tyrant, while Pharaoh was humiliated and drowned. Āsiyah was able to remain firm and steadfast in the face of torture, while Pharaoh caved at the first instance of danger. Āsiyah was given a home near Allah in Paradise, while Pharaoh will be in the Hellfire. Allah gives internal strength and dignity to those who follow His way, and who are humble and righteous. He makes examples of the oppressors by defeating them, and ultimately, they will be judged on the Day of Judgment by Allah. Part of living with this name is to strengthen ourselves internally through faith, as well as externally. It is to deeply feel the dignity that one has due to being a servant of al-'Azīz, and to behave accordingly. It means to be unwavering in strength and steadfastness because we know that our Lord is the Almighty – al-'Azīz.

He is the Mighty, the Invincible, and the Honorable.

- Al-Ḥakīm – The Most Wise (2:220)
- Al-Qawī – The Strong (11:66)
- Ar-Raḥīm – The Especially Merciful (26:9)
- Al-'Alīm – The All-Knowing (27:78)
- Al-Ghafūr – The All-Forgiving (35:38)
- Al-Ghaffār – The Perpetual Forgiver (52:28)

- Feeling weak, overburdened and up against difficult challenges.
- When you see someone being humiliated unjustly.
- If you find yourself feeling arrogant and above others.

Ya Azīz make us among those who rely upon Your power only, make us strong believers.

When do you feel weak and overpowered in life and how do you react to that situation? How might you remember al-'Azīz during these times to regain strength?

AL-JABBĀR

THE COMPELLER

'He is God: there is no god other than Him, the Controller, the Holy One, Source of Peace, Granter of Security, the Almighty, the Compeller, the Superior.' (59:23)

STORY

Sometimes we can feel shattered internally because of the hardships that we face. Sometimes there are others who hurt us and cause our hearts to break. Life can overwhelm us. When the Prophet ﷺ went to the city of Ta'if to seek the protection of its people, they turned him away in the most unbecoming way possible. This was after losing his beloved wife of 25 years and uncle who was like a father to him. He was broken, but he turned to the only One who could truly console him and mend what was broken. Al-Jabbār comforted him in that moment through a young boy who listened to him, He consoled him later through the miraculous journey of al-Isrā wal-Mirāj where he spoke directly to Allah, and He then gave him a community in Madina, and loving relationships. This shows us that al-Jabbār can mend in different ways, and He mends in the immediate and in the long-term. He mends through the kind act of a stranger, through an uplifting spiritual experience, and through slowly bringing in new people into our life - and more. And because the meaning of al-Jabbār is both mending and compelling, the other manifestation of this name is that He compels the oppressors, and those who 'break' others unjustly, through His might and His will.

MEANING
He is the One who can compel His servants through His might, and He can heal the hearts by repairing and mending them.

PAIRING
- Al-'Azīz - The Almighty (59:23)
- Al-Mutakabbir - The Superior (59:23)

SITUATION
- When you feel broken.
- Be wary of breaking others – hurting or oppressing them – because al-Jabbār may mend their hearts by compelling or overpowering you.
- When others need your help to mend them.

DU'A

Ya Jabbār, mend our hearts when we are broken and protect us from breaking the hearts of others.

REFLECTIVE QUESTION
Describe a time in your life when you felt internally broken, how did al-Jabbār restore you?

الْمُتَكَبِّر

AL-MUTAKABBIR

THE SUPERIOR

'He is God: there is no god other than Him, the Controller, the Holy One, Source of Peace, Granter of Security, the Almighty, the Compeller, the Superior.' (59:23)

STORY

When a human being is 'mutakabbir', he sees himself as above other people. The reason for thinking one is greater is usually due to superficial reasons, like wealth, status, ethnicity or other equally trivial reasons. This feeling eventually, if not immediately, leads to wronging and transgressing against others. Even if one thinks that they are better than others because of their religiosity (an ostensibly 'good' reason), this is a sign that they are not truly pious, because a pious person is focused on rectifying his or her own faults while excusing the faults of others. Whereas when we say that Allah is al-Mutakabbir, it is to remind and alert us that He actually possesses traits that are above all others, and thus we should humble ourselves before Him. Being arrogant - even slightly - is as though you are competing with Allah for this name. The irony is that Allah abases the one who is arrogant, and elevates the one who is humble.

He is the Proud, the Supreme, and the Truly Great. This name is unique in its positive connotations for Allah, as a human being who is 'mutakabbir' is arrogant.

- Al-Jabbār - The Compeller (59:23)

- When you start to feel haughty and to look down on people.
- When you see yourself above others, remember that this is a trait of Satan.
- One way of discovering 'hidden arrogance' is when someone corrects you and you think you are too good for the advice.

Ya Mutakabbir, guide our hearts and actions to humility towards You.

Is arrogance a trait that you have and what leads you to becoming arrogant? How can you cure this arrogance?

الخَالِق

AL-KHĀLIQ

THE CREATOR

'So blessed is Allah, the best of creators.' (23:14)

STORY

At-tafakkur (deep contemplation) is considered an act of worship and, for many of the righteous, it was preferable to other forms of voluntary worship. Why? Because reflecting deeply upon the creation of the heavens, the earth, and everything within can only lead to the One who made them: al-Khāliq. Before the Prophet ﷺ received revelation, he would go to the Cave of Hira to reflect. He would contemplate deeply the heavens and the earth. He was likely wondering how humans were brought to existence, who created us, and what our purpose is. And the first verses revealed to him were, 'Recite in the name of your Lord who created - Created man from a clinging substance.' (96:1-2) This was the answer. Everything that is created — even ourselves — is a sign that leads to the One who created: Allah al-Khāliq. If one takes out just a few minutes a day and sits and reflects on the sky, for instance, or how our eye functions, one cannot help but be awed and humbled by Allah. When you feel the warmth of the rays of the sun shining on you, or the cool drops of rain that fall on you, let that remind you that these are not random: these are created by al-Khāliq, and thus they have a purpose. Now take that to yourself: al-Khāliq created you, so what is your purpose? Finally, this name is not static - al-Khāliq creates in the present as well, and He can create ways out from our hardships, and new opportunities when it appears that there are none.

Allah is both al-Khāliq and al-Khallāq, which come from the same root. Al-Khāliq is He who determines what is to be brought into existence and does so, and al-Khallāq indicates the sheer quantity of what He creates.

- Al-'Alīm - The All-Knowing (15:86)
- Al-Bāri' - The Producer (59:24)
- Al-Muṣawwir - The Fashioner (59:24)

- When you look at the natural world.
- When you become consumed by the worldly life and the material, remember that you were created with a purpose. Allah asks us in the Qur'an, 'Then did you think that We created you uselessly and that to Us you would not be returned?' (23:115)
- When you feel you have lost a sense of purpose in life.

Ya Khāliq, guide us to remember You as the creator, and help us to live our true purpose in life.

How might you begin to cultivate a daily practice of reflecting upon the creation of Allah? Why did Allah create you?

AL-BĀRI'

THE PRODUCER

'He is Allah, the Creator, the Producer, the Fashioner; to Him belong the best names.' (59:24)

STORY

Have you ever reflected upon the different types of trees? Scientists have compiled a database of over 60,000 different tree species, and these are just what we know - imagine all the types of trees that we do not know about! The earth and all the diversity it contains is not something that happened by chance; it was created and manifested by al-Khāliq al-Bāri', who creates everything with purpose. Each tree gives us different types of timber, food, and medicine — though they are all trees, the small distinctions that differentiate them contain benefits for us - this is the creation of al-Bāri'. Now take a step back, and think of everything on this earth and how they are different from one another, each with its own purpose. This should encourage us to preserve and protect the environment and the biodiversity contained therein. Moreover, knowing that Allah has distinguished and differentiated between His creation should cause us to celebrate and honor our God-given differences; indeed, Allah says, 'O mankind, We have created you from a male and a female and made you into races and tribes, that you may know one another; indeed, the most noble of you in the sight of Allah are the most mindful (of Him) among you; indeed, Allah is All-Knowing, All-Aware.' (49:13) The differences in our languages and colors should cause us to want to know one another, and not see ourselves as above one another, as the only thing that makes us better or worse is our God-consciousness, and only Allah can judge that.

His name al-Bāri' means that He manifests things into existence, whether from non-existence or pre-existing matter, He distinguishes the created beings from each other, and is He Himself distant from any blemish.

- Al-Khāliq - The Creator (59:24)
- Al-Muṣawwir - The Fashioner (59:24)

- When we hear about climate change and are tempted to just switch off, we should remember that because of what we are doing, we are losing precious species that Allah has created.

Ya Bāri' help us ponder Your creations and appreciate them.

Have you ever pondered the subtle differences between the various species that al-Bāri' has created?

الْمُصَوِّر

AL-MUṢAWWIR

THE FASHIONER

'He is Allah, the Creator, the Inventor, the Fashioner; to Him belong the best names.' (59:24)

STORY

This name comes after the names al-Khāliq and al-Bāri' in Sūrat al-Ḥashr (59:24), as though Allah is taking us through the different steps of creation, showing us that He is there every step of the way. He creates from nothing (al-Khāliq), manifests into existence from nothing as well as from what He has created, distinguishing between creation (al-Bāri'), and fashions and shapes everything Himself. One of the best ways to connect to this name is to look at the development of a fetus in the womb, and how the facial features evolve. Indeed, when we look at our own fingertips and realize that every single human being has a unique fingerprint, this should make us feel special; Allah has made you unique. When we look at our own faces, we should remember that Allah Himself has fashioned us, and indeed He has made all of us in our different shapes. Our diversity is a sign that leads us to al-Muṣawwir; thus, no one should ever feel as though they are above anyone else because of how they look or their ethnicity – all were made by al-Muṣawwir. Similarly, we should reject beauty standards that seek to alter the way Allah has fashioned us - He created all of us with an inherent beauty, and it is enough that He has fashioned us Himself.

MEANING
He is the One who gives everything its form, thus He is the Fashioner.

PAIRING
- Al-Khāliq - The Creator (59:24)
- Al-Bāri' - the Producer (59:24)

SITUATION
- Whenever you feel unattractive or ugly because of dubious human standards, remember that you have been fashioned by Allah.
- When you look at others, see them as beautiful beings fashioned by al-Muṣawwir.
- When you feel that you are not special, remember that Allah has fashioned you Himself.

DU'A

Ya Muṣawwir, allow us to be thankful for the way in which you made us.

REFLECTIVE QUESTION
Allah is the Creator, the Producer and the Fashioner, what do each of these Names now mean to you?

الغَفَّار

AL-GHAFFĀR

THE PERPETUAL FORGIVER

'Ask forgiveness of your Lord. Indeed, He is ever a Perpetual Forgiver.' (71:10)

STORY

One of the tricks of Satan is to make us feel that there is no hope for us, particularly when we mess up in a major way. Malik bin Dinar, a great scholar, was once someone who lived a depraved lifestyle. He committed many of the major sins; but not only did he know that Allah is al-Ghaffār and would forgive his serious blunders if he sincerely repented, he went on to become a scholar, benefitting us to this day. This is an example that not only does Allah forgive your major and even public indiscretions, but you can be better than you were before. So whenever you mess up in a way that you feel you cannot forgive yourself, remember that Allah is telling you He is al-Ghaffār, which means by definition that He forgives the major sins. All He requires of you is to turn back to Him, stop the sin or sincerely try to stop, seek His forgiveness, and to do your best to not return to the sin.

MEANING

Al-Ghaffār not only continuously forgives sins, but He forgives even the greatest sins.

PAIRING

- Al-'Azīz - The Almighty (39:5)

SITUATION

- When you feel ashamed because you committed a grave sin that you never thought you would.
- When you feel that you cannot forgive yourself.
- When you are looking down on someone who is committing sins, Allah's forgiveness encompasses them too.

DU'A

Ya Ghaffār, forgive the sins that I don't remember and the sins that I didn't even consider as sins, the sins of the past and the sins of the future.

REFLECTIVE QUESTION

How can you cultivate a daily wird (routine) of asking Allah for forgiveness?

الْقَهَّار

AL-QAHHĀR

THE PREVAILING

'To whom belongs [all] sovereignty this Day? To Allah,
the One, the Prevailing.' (40:16)

STORY

Qarun tyrannized his people, even though he was of the people of Musa (as). Despite being advised by those with knowledge to desist from his tyranny and do good with what he had been given, he insisted upon the transgressions, even going as far as to say that he was only given it due to knowledge that he had. The result? Allah says, 'And We caused the earth to swallow him and his home' (28:81) This is one manifestation of His name al-Qahhār, where an oppressor is physically taken down and one witnesses clearly his overpowering. But al-Qahhār prevails over those who oppress in different ways, not only materially. If a transgressor seems outwardly powerful and able to hurt those weaker than him, remember that al-Qahhār might overpower him internally through ensuring that this person never has internal peace. Thus, seeing injustice in the world should not cause us to despair or to think that those who cause harm to others have 'won'. Even if we do not witness the fall of tyrants and oppressors in this world, Allah reminds us that on the Day of Judgment, we will know to whom all sovereignty belongs: 'To whom belongs [all] sovereignty this Day? To Allah, the One, the Prevailing.' (40:16) They will be overpowered on that day.

Al-Qahhār is constantly prevailing over His creation through His will and might.

- Al-Wāhid - The One (12:39)

- When we see oppression, we should not despair, but rather know that Allah overpowers transgressors in different ways.
- Part of knowing this name and manifesting it in a human sense is to overpower your nafs (lower self).

Ya Qahhār, allow us to overpower our nafs and protect us from others who want to overpower us.

Think of a time when you were oppressed and a time when you perhaps oppressed others. What would you have done differently?

الوَهّاب

AL-WAHHĀB

THE BESTOWER OF GIFTS

'Our Lord, let not our hearts deviate after You have guided us and grant us from Yourself mercy. Indeed, You are the Bestower (al-Wahhab).' (3:8)

STORY

Think of the last time you received a gift and how that made you feel. You likely felt warm inside, and affection for one that gave you the gift. You probably also felt loved or seen by the person who gave you the gift. You might have even been a little embarrassed because the gift was so generous, or it was from someone you have not had that much contact with lately. Now take all of those feelings and apply them to the gifts you receive from Allah. What are these gifts? The definition of a gift is something that is given without compensation. So, they are in the everyday things that we fail to notice that Allah gives to everyone – the air that we breathe, our lungs that function, loved ones around us. These are all gifts that we did not do anything to receive. But gifts are also more specific to us. A gift can be through something that comes to you unexpectedly, like a trip you so badly needed or even an umrah. And it can be simpler than that too. It can be the random stranger that pays for your coffee, or reassurance from someone when you feel worried. All of these are manifestations of specific gifts that al-Wahhāb gives to you. And what does the giving of a gift mean? It means care for you, it means you are seen, and it means love. Think of all of that the next time you reflect upon Allah's gifts.

Al-Wahhāb is the Gift Giver, who constantly showers His servants with gifts.

Al-'Azīz - The Almighty (38:9)

SITUATION

- When something good happens to you with or without very little effort on your part.
- When you look at your children or any of your loved ones, remember that they are gifts from al-Wahhāb.
- Give gifts in order to engender love, as the Prophet ﷺ advised.

DU'A

Ya Wahhāb, make us of those who are grateful for Your gifts and use them to please You.

REFLECTIVE QUESTION

Write down the gifts that you believe you have overlooked or taken for granted. How many can you count? How will you show gratitude?

الرَّزَّاق

AR-RAZZĀQ

THE PROVIDER

'Indeed, it is Allah who is the [continual] Provider, the firm possessor of strength.' (51:58)

STORY

Every single being on earth needs their provision. We all work in order to be able to provide basic needs for ourselves and our families, in addition to the extras that we require. When our earnings are limited, this causes us to worry about the future. When the economy is down, we wonder how we will find a new job. When our expenses go up, we wonder how we will cope. Ar-Razzāq teaches us to look to Him as the ultimate Provider, while everything we described were simply outward manifestations. He has apportioned for us our provision and everyone will get that which was apportioned for him or her. Knowing that He is ar-Razzāq means knowing that He will provide for us and indeed He continually provides for us and for every living being; not simply sustenance itself, but the means of sustenance. This has implications for us: first, knowing that He is ar-Razzāq does not mean sitting back and waiting for the provision to arrive at our doors. Rather, it is using the means that He has provided in order to obtain our sustenance. Second, it is to shun forbidden (ḥarām) means to obtain our livelihoods. Knowing that He is ar-Razzāq means that we know that our sustenance is from Him, and not what appears to be the means on the surface. These forbidden means are a test and temptation, forcing us to ask ourselves: Do I trust in ar-Razzāq or do I trust in what He has prohibited? Indeed, taking the route deemed illegitimate by Him can prevent our supplication from being responded to. Sins can also prevent one's rizq from reaching them. If you find yourself wondering whether there is truly a link between our deeds and the provision we receive, as many people who use wrongful means appear to receive much wealth, this is because we fail to conceive that provision is of many types. Those who use unethical means to increase their wealth may receive material rizq, but Allah may deny them their spiritual rizq.

Ar-Razzāq is constantly providing His servants with that which benefits them physically and spiritually.

- When you are applying for a job or running a business.
- When times are tough and it feels that your provision is limited.
- Do not neglect your spiritual sustenance: just like we go out and seek our material rizq, we should be just as diligent in seeking our spiritual rizq.

Ya Razzāq, make us of those who are content with Your provisions, guide us to work hard and use Your provisions wisely.

Describe a time when you perhaps felt that your sustenance was low, how did ar-Razzāq provide for you during that time?

الفَتَّاح

AL-FATTĀḤ

THE OPENER, THE JUDGE

*'Our Lord, decide (iftah) between us and our people in truth,
and You are the best of those who give decision (al-Fattah).'*
(7:89)

STORY

We all find ourselves at some point in life being stuck, or standing before proverbial doors that are closed. Something that we want so much seems so far out of reach no matter how hard we try. Knowing that Allah is al-Fattāḥ is knowing that He opens that which is closed. What this means for us is that we have faith that when we work our hardest with the means we have, we know that Allah will open the doors for us. Sometimes it might not be the door we are knocking, but because He is al-Fattāḥ al-'Alīm (the All-Knowing Opener), He opens the doors which are best for us. What we learn from the story of the Prophet Yusuf (as) is that sometimes an 'opening' looks like a closed door to begin with. When Yusuf (as) was rescued from the well that he was left in by his brothers, he was sold into slavery. Put yourself in his place: this would definitely not feel like an opening to you! It might even feel like Allah is closing the door in your face, because you are moving farther away from your family and you are moving from ease to hardship. But that was actually the first step to the opening. The dark well was an opening because at the end of the story, he is reunited with his family in the best circumstances. So have faith.

MEANING

Al-Fattāḥ is the One who opens everything that is closed, be that a difficulty through easing it, a problem through solving it, and the truth through revealing it.

PAIRING

■ Al-'Alīm - The All-Knowing (34:26)

SITUATION

■ When you face hurdles in life, and feel like all the doors are closed to you.
■ When you embark on something unknown.
■ When it seems that truth is obscured, ask al-Fattāḥ to reveal the truth.

DU'A

Ya Fattāḥ, open for us the doors and the truth to all that is good in this life.

REFLECTIVE QUESTION

How stuck do you feel in your life right now? Describe a time when you felt stuck and al-Fattāḥ helped to open the right doors for you?

العَلِيم

AL-'ALĪM

THE ALL-KNOWING

'And let not their statements sadden you, Indeed, all might belongs to Allah; He is the All-Hearing, the All-Knowing.'
(1:1)

STORY

We all desire to be understood. And some of us may have loved ones who understand us, but few of us can say that someone knows everything about us. Allah is al-'Alīm — He knows our hopes and our desires. He knows the thoughts that cross our minds. He knows the intentions we have kept hidden and the words and deeds we have made public. On one level, this should comfort us. Allah is al-'Alīm, who knows everything about us, and still invites us to return to Him, still grants us His love, and still bestows upon us His mercy. His door is always open to us, not because He does not know us, but precisely because He does. He knows our struggles. He knows when we have been wronged, and we can take comfort in all of that. On another level, this should teach us to guard what we do in secret. We might say things on social media because we are hiding behind an anonymous account, but Allah knows all that we put out into the world. We should care about what He knows, rather than what people think they know. Finally, knowing He is al-'Alīm should inspire in us awe as well as humility. Awe because of the vastness of His knowledge, and humility because no matter how much we believe we know, Allah knows more. This should make us realize that no matter how much knowledge we acquire, there is more to be known and understood. Our knowledge should not cause us to be arrogant over others, but rather should make us realize how much we do not know, and how much more there is to learn.

MEANING

Al-'Alīm is the All-Knowing, the One who knows everything: what is secret and what is in the open, what is hidden and what is revealed, what was, what is, and what will be.

PAIRING

- Al-Shākir – Appreciative (2:158)
- Al-Wāsi – All-Embracing (3:73)
- Al-Ḥalīm – Forbearing (4:12)
- As-Samī – All-Hearing (5:76)
- Al-Khabīr – All-Aware (31:34)

SITUATION

- When you are under hardship or feel no-one understands you.
- When you want to do something that you know is wrong, thinking you can hide it from people.
- If you have been wronged or misinterpreted by others.

DU'A

Ya 'Alīm, you know what is in my heart, You know the desires, the struggles, the anxieties I am enduring, bestow upon me Your guidance.

REFLECTIVE QUESTION

Describe a time when you felt alone and that no-one was able to understand how you are feeling. How can you call upon al-'Alīm during these times?

MEMORIZATION LIST

Ar-Raḥmān	1	○
Ar-Raḥīm	2	○
Al-Malik	3	○
Al-Quddūs	4	○
As-Salām	5	○
Al-Mu'min	6	○
Al-Muhaymin	7	○
Al-'Azīz	8	○
Al-Jabbār	9	○
Al-Mutakabbir	10	○
Al-Khāliq	11	○
Al-Bāri'	12	○
Al-Muṣawwir	13	○
Al-Ghaffār	14	○
Al-Qahhār	15	○
Al-Wahhāb	16	○
Ar-Razzāq	17	○
Al-Fattāḥ	18	○
Al-'Alīm	19	○
Al-Qābiḍ	**20**	○
Al-Bāsiṭ	**21**	○
Al-Khāfiḍ	22	○
Ar-Rāfi'	23	○
Al-Muizz	24	○
Al-Mudhill	25	○
As-Samī'	26	○
Al-Baṣīr	27	○
Al-Ḥakam	28	○
Al-'Adl	29	○
Al-Laṭīf	30	○
Al-Khabīr	31	○
Al-Ḥalīm	32	○
Al-'Aẓīm	33	○
Al-Ghafūr	34	○
Ash-Shakūr	35	○
Al-'Alī	36	○
Al-Kabīr	37	○
Al-Ḥafīz	38	○
Al-Muqīt	39	○
Al-Ḥasīb	40	○
Al-Jalīl	41	○
Al-Karīm	42	○
Ar-Raqīb	43	○
Al-Mujīb	44	○
Al-Wāsi'	45	○
Al-Ḥakīm	46	○
Al-Wadūd	47	○
Al-Majīd	48	○
Al-Bā'ith	49	○
Ash-Shahīd	50	○
Al-Ḥaqq	51	○
Al-Wakīl	52	○
Al-Qawī	53	○
Al-Matīn	54	○
Al-Walī	55	○
Al-Ḥamīd	56	○
Al-Muḥsī	57	○
Al-Mubdi'	58	○
Al-Mu'īd	59	○
Al-Muḥyī	60	○
Al-Mumīt	61	○
Al-Ḥayy	62	○
Al-Qayyūm	63	○
Al-Wājid	64	○
Al-Mājid	65	○
Al-Wāhid	66	○
Al-Aḥad	67	○
Aṣ-Ṣamad	68	○
Al-Qādir	69	○
Al-Qadīr	70	○
Al-Muqtadir	71	○
Al-Muqaddim	72	○
Al-Mu'akhir	73	○
Al-Awwal	74	○
Al-Ākhir	75	○
Az-Ẓāhir	76	○
Al-Bāṭin	77	○
Al-Wālī	78	○
Al-Muta'āl	79	○
Al-Barr	80	○
At-Tawwāb	81	○
Al-Muntaqim	82	○
Al-'Afuww	83	○
Ar-Ra'ūf	84	○
Mālik al-Mulk	85	○
Dhū al-Jalāl wa al-Ikrām	86	○
Al-Muqsiṭ	87	○
Al-Jāmi'	88	○
Al-Ghanī	89	○
Al-Mughnī	90	○
Al-Māni'	91	○
Ad-Ḍārr	92	○
An-Nāfi'	93	○
An-Nūr	94	○
Al-Hādī	95	○
Al-Badī'	96	○
Al-Bāqī	97	○
Al-Wārith	98	○
Ar-Rashīd	99	○
Aṣ-Ṣabūr	100	○
Allāh	101	○

القابِض الباسِط

AL-QĀBIḌ
AL-BĀSIṬ

HE WHO CONTRACTS, HE WHO EXPANDS

The Prophet ﷺ said: 'Indeed, God is the Price-Setter, the One who takes away (al-Qabid) and gives abundantly (al-Basit).' (Ibn Majah)

STORY

The manifestations of qabḍ and basṭ are many, and we all have a relationship with al-Qābiḍ al-Bāsiṭ as we experience the highs and lows of life. Knowing the purpose of the highs and lows is what enables us to appreciate these names of Allah. At times, our souls feel constricted and life feels heavy. There may be reasons that we know of, or causes that we cannot pinpoint. But every feeling of discomfort that is met with patience and perseverance results in our elevation through forgiveness from Allah. Knowing that He is al-Qābiḍ is to know that any discomfort has a purpose. And just like He is al-Qābiḍ, He is al-Bāsiṭ, who can expand for us after restriction. If there are deep reasons for the negative feelings we are experiencing, it is imperative to go to someone who can help, such as a counsellor or a therapist. These means are from Allah, al-Bāsiṭ. Moreover, sometimes our provision is constricted. We may be working extremely hard but still our sustenance seems to be limited. Knowing that Allah is al-Qābiḍ is to know that when He restricts our provision it is for a reason: perhaps He is alerting us to the fact that our earnings are from religiously impermissible means and thus we find no pleasure in what little wealth we have; perhaps it is to remind us to be more concerned with our Hereafter if chasing after worldly wealth has made us forget our ultimate purpose; and perhaps it is to test our reaction to being restricted in our wealth. But knowing He is al-Qābiḍ is to be equally sure that He is al-Bāsiṭ; therefore, there will be eventual expansion and giving, and ultimate expansion in Paradise.

Al-Qābiḍ al-Bāsiṭ is the One who contracts and expands, constricting our provision in certain instances and increasing it in others, seizing our lives (in death) or releasing them, and compressing our souls and expanding them.

- When you feel constricted in progress and you need help with mental or emotional difficulties
- When you feel abundant in progress and you feel you need to protect yourself to withstand periods of restriction.

Ya Qābiḍ, Ya Bāsiṭ, for You Alone is all praise, none can restrict what You expand, and none can expand what You restrict.

Describe a time when something that was very close to your heart was taken away from you. How did you react at that time? How do you think the situation could've been dealt while incorporating this du'a?

الخَافِض الرَّافِع

AL-KHĀFIḌ AR-RĀFI'

THE ABASER, THE EXALTER

'We elevate in rank whoever We will.' (12:76)

STORY

When we look at the world around us, we see people 'elevated' for different reasons, as well as 'lowered'. Some are elevated in a worldly sense by their wealth, status, or any other standard that is deemed important in this life. Others are perceived to be lower because of their lack of means. Allah al-Khāfiḍ ar-Rāfi' shows us that He raises and lowers whomever He wills, but that worldly status tells us nothing about one's internal state or one's status with Allah. Thus, these names teach us not to be deceived by one's outward status in this world, and to pay attention to what truly elevates and what truly abases. Allah may raise someone outwardly in this world, but this person is abased spiritually because they use that elevation for that which Allah hates, and vice versa. The sunnah of life also shows that those who were once raised are eventually lowered. When it comes to us, we must remember that there is never a moment when we are obeying Allah except that we are elevated spiritually and with Him, and this should comfort us if we encounter opposition from other people. We should remember that humbling ourselves before Allah and resisting feelings of arrogance is actually what causes us to be elevated by ar-Rāfi'. Moreover, internally, when we do something wrong, the conscience that Allah has placed within us causes us to feel uncomfortable, low, and abased. Al-Khāfiḍ has placed this system in us so that we stay away from those deeds. On the other hand, when we do good, we feel uplifted. And that is ar-Rāfi' raising our spirits.

Al-Khāfiḍ ar-Rāfi is He who lowers and abases the wrongdoers and oppressors, and elevates the righteous.

- When you feel jealous of what others have materially.
- If you find yourself feeling arrogant for whatever reason, remember that Allah raises the humble, and while He humbles the arrogant.
- If you feel down that you have not reached a high position in a worldly sense, remember that al-Khāfiḍ ar-Rāfi is the Most Wise. Focus on elevating yourself in Paradise.

Ya Khāfiḍ Ya Rāfi, elevate us with your obedience and do not lower us through disobedience.

Compare your worldly state and actions with your internal state and worship, are they in sync?

الْمُعِز الْمُذِل

AL-MUIZZ
AL-MUDHILL

THE HONORER, THE HUMBLER

'Say, "O Allah, Master of the dominion, You grant dominion to whomever You will and You strip dominion from whomever you will, and You honor whomever you will and You humiliate whomever you will; in Your hand is all goodness. You are indeed All-Powerful over everything.' (3:26)

STORY

Most human beings want to feel honored. Because of this desire, what can happen is that people seek what they perceive to be honor outside of them. Attention is misinterpreted as honor and respect. And if we search for this sense of dignity outside of us, our standards for honor and dignity are naturally shaped by those external forces. But Allah tells us that He is al-Muizz al-Mudhill, which means that only He truly honors and only He humiliates. If honor and dignity are found with Him, should we not then reorient our standards to what He loves? Should we not dress, behave, and speak in a way that He has told us dignified, rather than what society has told us? If we do not pay attention to the desire of the nafs for approval from people, we might even justify acting in an undignified way. Moreover, when we look around us and find those who want power and influence committing evil acts in order to achieve that power and influence, and indeed oppressing those who want to live in Allah's way, have no doubt that al-Muizz al-Mudhill will honor those who obey, and will humiliate those who oppress.

Al-Muizz Al-Mudhill is the One who gives honor and dignity to the righteous, and who humiliates and humbles the wretched.

SITUATION

- If you feel tempted to speak or act in a way that would make you accepted in society but that you know is displeasing to Him, find strength in these names of Allah, and know that He honors those who do the right thing for Him.

DU'A

Ya Muizz, honor us in this life and the next through closeness to You, and do not humiliate us on the Day of Reckoning.

REFLECTIVE QUESTION

Are you working towards gaining honour and dignity from the people or from Allah?

AS-SAMĪ

THE ALL-HEARING

'Thereupon his Lord responded to him and diverted their plotting away from him; indeed, He is the All-Hearing, the All-Knowing.' (12:34)

STORY

When Allah gives Himself a name and reveals it to us, it is because this name is important for our relationship with Him, and indeed tells us about ourselves and how intimately Allah knows us. All of us desire to be heard and understood. We find comfort in the one who listens to us, yet we do not always find someone who will take the time to hear us. While we could turn to people, Allah reminds us that He is as-Samī – the All-Hearing. So, while we might find comfort in speaking to our friends and loved ones, we should find more comfort in the One who has named Himself as-Samī, telling us that He is always there to hear us. When you are alone, when you wish to talk about your troubles or express gratitude for your day, know that He is there, listening to you. Another crucial understanding of this name is to guard our speech because we know Allah is listening. When we are with those whom we respect, we ensure that what we say is respectful and appropriate. And Allah is always with us – so this should motivate us to refine our speech. Finally, when the Prophet Musa (as) expressed His fear to Allah as he was about to face Pharaoh, Allah reminded Musa that He is with him, hearing and seeing. Whenever you are facing a difficult situation, remember that He is with you too, hearing and seeing.

As-Samīʿ is the One who hears everything, and what is said out loud is the same to Him as what is whispered (and what is more subtle than that). He hears our unspoken words and the prayers trapped in our hearts, as well as our speech and supplications.

- Al-Qarīb - The Near One (34:50)
- Al-'Alīm - The All-Knowing (49:1)
- Al-Baṣīr - The All-Seeing (58:1)

- When you feel the urge to say something that is not appropriate or is backbiting.
- Accustom yourself to speaking as though you are in front of someone you respect and love deeply, because you are always before as-Samīʿ.

Ya Samī, You hear what is in our hearts, so grant us that which we love and is good for us, and enable us to purify our speech, so that we never utter what you dislike.

Do you invoke Allah's name and worship Him in a manner that you would like Him to hear?

البَصِير

AL-BAṢĪR

THE ALL-SEEING

*'...for He is with you wherever you may be. And Allah is
All-Seeing of what you do.'* (57:4)

STORY

When we say that Allah is al-Baṣīr, we might wonder what the difference is between Him knowing what we do and seeing what we do. Are they not the same? However, the way we conceptualize knowing and seeing is very different. Saying that someone 'knows' something does not tell us anything about the time and space of that knowledge. You might know something about me, but it doesn't require you to be present with me in the same space to know it. When we say that someone sees something, however, it implies that we are together at the same moment. For example, if you had done something bad, and someone else knew of what you had done, you might feel uncomfortable or embarrassed. But you might be able to ignore it because that person might be far from you and you do not have to face them. However, if they saw you in the same moment you did that wrong thing, these feelings would be intensified. It might even prevent you from doing something wrong because you know that someone is watching you. This also applies to good things. If you are competing in a race, knowing that your loved one is there watching you, as opposed to simply knowing you are competing, likely makes you feel loved and supported, which motivates you to do your best. Similarly, when we know that Allah is al-Baṣīr, we understand that He sees us and is with us in this -- and every -- moment. He sees the good we do and the bad. He sees us when we struggle to wake up for fajr prayer, yet still persevere in doing so. This should comfort us because we know that we are under His watchful eye at every moment, as well as encourage us to be vigilant over our actions. Moreover, because al-Baṣīr's seeing is wholly different to human 'seeing', He also sees our inward reality. Just like we polish ourselves outwardly because we know we will be meeting with people, we should polish our heart inwardly knowing that Allah sees; for Allah, His seeing of our inward and outward is the same. He also sees our internal struggles that are invisible to the people. Thus, knowing al-Baṣīr should make us feel seen; because we are.

MEANING

Al-Baṣīr is the All-Seeing, who sees what is tinier than the atom, that which we can see and that which is hidden from our sight, the outward and the inward.

PAIRING

* As-Samī' - All-Hearing (58:1)
* Al-Khabīr - All-Aware (35:31)

SITUATION

* When you do good, get excited about the fact that al-Baṣīr is seeing you.
* When you are planning to commit a sin.

DU'A

Ya Baṣīr, help us to purify ourselves internally and externally so that what You see from us is pleasing to You.

REFLECTIVE QUESTION

Imagine you were looking down upon yourself for today, how would you view yourself? How would Allah have seen you today?

AL-ḤAKAM

THE JUDGE

‘ Indeed, Allah is the Arbitrator (al-Hakam) and to Him is the judgment.’ (Abu Dawud)

STORY

Many people find the concept of divine decree confusing. Does that mean that everything is written or do we have a say in the matter? But delving into these questions is a distraction because we will not be asked about Allah's decree on the Day of Judgment. We will be asked, however, what we did with the means around us and how we dealt with and reacted to those things outside of our control. The latter has to do with our understanding of al-Ḥakam. The things we know are decreed are those things that transpire that cannot be changed. Knowing it is from al-Ḥakam is to accept what happened, but also learning from it for our future. It is to 'Know that if the whole world were to gather together in order to help you, they would not be able to help you except if Allah had written so. And if the whole world were to gather together in order to harm you, they would not harm you except if Allah had written so. The pens have been lifted, and the pages are dry.' (Tirmidhī) The other meaning of al-Ḥakam is that He has made certain rules and told us to live by them – these are also from His decree. Knowing that certain established laws are from al-Ḥakam, who only decrees out of His knowledge and His wisdom, means knowing that even when we do not understand, we know that the rules He has decreed for us are what is best for us in any given moment. Thus, we should study and familiarize ourselves with the obligations He has prescribed for us. Finally, al-Ḥakam is the One who will judge on the Day of Judgment, so we should ask ourselves: how would I like to appear before Him?

Al-Ḥakam is the Judge, who decrees out of His wisdom, mercy, and justice, and whose decree no one can overturn.

- When you feel oppressed or see oppression done to others.
- When you lament on things in the past you cannot change.

Ya Ḥakam, make me content with your decree, and allow me to accept my circumstances and focus on my present and future.

Do you get stuck in or worked up over what happened in the past? How does knowing that Allah is al-Ḥakam change the way you view the past?

'And the word of your Lord has been fulfilled in truth and in justice.' (6:115)

STORY

How is Allah al-'Adl when we see so much injustice in the world? This is a question many people ask. But we have to always remember two things when contemplating this name and attribute: first, we are in this world to strive. Thus, part of our mission as ones who submit to al-'Adl is to establish justice – for everyone, and even if it were against ourselves (whether that is the individual or the collective self). Indeed, numerous verses in the Qur'an and sayings of the Prophet ﷺ remind us that Allah will never wrong anyone, and that we should establish justice on this earth and between us. The scholar Ibn Taymiyyah is reported to have said that Allah will protect a just nation even if they are not believers, and He would bring down an unjust nation even if they were believers. Thus, the injustice that we see around us is a call for us to end oppression and establish justice. Allah also says in the Qur'an: 'O you who have believed, be persistently standing firm for Allah, witnesses in justice, and do not let the hatred of a people prevent you from being just. Be just; that is nearer to righteousness. And fear Allah; indeed, Allah is Acquainted with what you do.' (5:8). Second, this world is only one part of the life that we live, and it is the shorter part. The Hereafter is for eternity. Thus, though we may be striving for justice to the degree that we are able, it hurts us when it appears that tyranny has won. But this is why al-'Adl constantly reminds us of the Hereafter: ultimate justice will be served there. No oppressor will escape, and those who were wronged will be recompensed.

Al-'Adl is the Most Just, who only acts with justice, who made oppression forbidden for Him and forbade it for others.

SITUATION

- Always stand for justice, in the big and the small when you see injustice in the world.
- When you see injustice but feel helpless in knowing what to do.

DU'A

Ya Adl, enable me to establish justice, and prevent me from being of the unjust.

REFLECTIVE QUESTION

Are you just in your treatment of others? Do you advocate for justice even if it would harm your interests?

TRACE

اللَّطِيف

AL-LAṬĪF

THE BENEVOLENT, THE SUBTLE

'Indeed, my Lord is Subtle in fulfilling whatever He wills'
(12:100)

STORY

Signs of love and care are not simple in grand gestures; they are usually found in the more mundane and in the subtle interactions of everyday life. We are all recipients of subtle blessings that we might not take notice of: the smile of a stranger when we are down, or the phone call from a friend who wants to ask about how we are. It can even be in gentle admonishment that makes us better. These are all manifestations of His name al-Laṭīf – He who is with us through every step of the way, who knows the elusive realities of our hearts, and He gently sends us what we need. Perhaps a random person you met at a conference ended up helping you get a job later on, or introduced you to someone who is now your dearest friend. Indeed, al-Laṭīf's manifestations are all over the universe and not just in our personal lives. He tells us, 'Have you not considered how God sends water down from the sky and the next morning the earth becomes green? God is truly most subtle, all aware.' (22:63) Those things we take for granted are from His gentleness and subtlety.

MEANING
Al-Laṭīf is He who is Benevolent and Subtle with His servants.

PAIRING
▪ Al-Khabīr – All-Aware (67:14)

SITUATION
▪ When you feel ungrateful.
▪ When you feel a gentle breeze or are calmed by the sound of the sea.
▪ Manifest that gentleness and kindness with other people.

DU'A

Ya Laṭīf, bestow upon me your gentleness and enable me to recognize it and be gentle with others.

REFLECTIVE QUESTION
Think about the subtle blessings in your life that you did not acknowledge as significant, but when you reflect now, you realize that they helped lift your spirits or helped you along your path.

AL-KHABĪR

THE TOTALLY AWARE

'... it is God who is All-Knowing and All-Aware.' (31:34)

STORY

Most people only see our outward, both what is good and what is bad from it. Those we live with or are close to are more intimately aware of those parts of us we do not show to the outside world. But no one truly knows the state of our hearts. Al-Khabīr is the One who is aware of all of the secrets of our hearts, the intentions behind our deeds, the way we truly feel about others and what we harbor for them or against them, and our silent hopes, needs and desires. We cannot put up a front before al-Khabīr. On the one hand, there is comfort in this because we know that He truly knows us, and knows our internal struggles. Thus, the whole world and our loved ones may be oblivious to certain hardships we are facing, but al-Khabīr is with us, taking what we go through into account. On the other hand, it should force us to rectify ourselves internally because He sees the reality of the state of our hearts. We can pretend in front of people, but we can never pretend in front of Allah. So we should work on our internal state just as much – if not more – than we do on our outer actions.

MEANING

Al-Khabīr is the One whose knowledge encompasses the inner nature of things; thus He not only knows our actions, but also the state of our hearts.

PAIRING

- Al-Ḥakīm – Most Wise (6:73)
- Al-Baṣīr – All-Seeing (35:31)
- Al-'Alīm – All-Knowing (66:3)
- Al-Laṭīf – The Subtle (67:14)

SITUATION

- When you feel a lack of sweetness and peace in your worship.
- Work on knowing yourself so that you can understand your internal realities, what motivates you, so that you can improve the state of your heart.
- Remember that it is futile to try to impress people outwardly, rather it is important to 'impress' Allah.

DU'A

Ya Khabīr, You know what others do not and You are aware of what is in my heart, so help me to rectify my heart for Your sake.

REFLECTIVE QUESTION

Do you know your inner self? What is one thing you could rectify about yourself internally?

AL-ḤALĪM

'Indeed, those of you who turned away on the day when the two armies met—it was Satan who caused them to backslide on account of some of what they had earned. But Allah has most surely pardoned them, for Allah is indeed Oft-Forgiving, Forbearing.' (3:155)

STORY

We all appreciate being given a second chance. We appreciate not being sent to detention in school or being given the opportunity to apply for a position even after missing the deadlines. We appreciate the traffic officer who forgoes giving us a ticket for parking in the wrong place. These opportunities, if we recognize them as such, should push us to do better so that we are not put in the same position again, as well as feeling gratitude for the one who gave us that opportunity. Al-Ḥalīm is like this with us and more, every single day. We all make mistakes, some minor and some major, at different points in our lives. Many times, we do not see an immediate consequence to our actions and we have to be cognizant of the fact that this is deliberate. Knowing al-Ḥalīm is knowing that Allah gives us opportunities to turn back to Him and to rectify ourselves; this is the purpose of the forbearance. And if we do suffer negative consequences as a result of bad things we might have done, we need to remember that this too is from al-Ḥalīm; how so? If Allah were to be so forbearing with us that it causes us to be heedless, then this adversely affects our Hereafter because we will be judged for those misdeeds. But if Allah alerts us in the form of a punishment or test, it is precisely so that we can rectify our actions in this life so that we do not have to contend with them on the Day of Judgment. Thus, in all is good, and in all is an opportunity to return to Allah.

MEANING

Al-Ḥalīm is the Forbearing One, who is unperturbed, and who is never quick or hasty to punish.

PAIRING

- Al-Ghanī – Self-Sufficient (2:263),
- Al-Ghafūr - The Oft-Forgiving (3:155)
- Al-'Alīm – All-Knowing (4:12)
- Ash-Shakūr – Appreciative (64:17)

SITUATION

- When you feel far from Allah due to sins you know you should not be committing, but continue to receive blessings, recognize that this is from al-Ḥalīm in order that you might reflect on your actions and return to Him.
- Be forbearing with others when they make mistakes, just like you love for Allah to be forbearing with you.

DU'A

Ya Ḥalīm, never deprive us from Yourself and from giving us the gracious chances to turn back to You.

REFLECTIVE QUESTION

How is your current state of forbearance? How do you think you can improve?

العَظيم

AL-'AẒĪM

THE TREMENDOUS

'...He is the Most High, the Tremendous.' (2:255)

STORY

Knowing this name should induce in us a sense of awe. When we reflect on the created world, this should immediately lead us to His name al-'Aẓīm because this world and everything in it is a testimony to His greatness. Indeed, knowing that He is al-'Aẓīm reminds us that He is greater than any obstacle we can ever face, and thus our hearts can be strengthened by Him in order to face the difficulties we encounter. Coming to this realization – that He is the Tremendous, the Truly Great – should lead us to something else: since He is al-'Aẓīm, He is the only One who can define what true greatness is for us. We would not trust someone who is dressed as a football player to teach us football even though he looks the part, over an expert in football. The latter has achieved 'greatness' in his realm, while the former is simply playing the part. Allah is far above any analogy, but this should drive the point home that only what He defines as great has that status, and what He has deemed reprehensible can never be great no matter how beautiful the façade is. This is just to remind us that when some worldly standards tell us to do or be something that Allah has deemed unacceptable, we should trust al-'Aẓīm's standards.

MEANING

Al-'Aẓīm is the Tremendous and the Greatest, who encompasses all forms of greatness at every level one can conceive of.

PAIRING

▪ Al-'Alī – Most High (42:4)

SITUATION

▪ Whenever you feel 'great' in a way that makes you feel above others, humble yourself before al-'Aẓīm.

▪ Reflect upon the creation as a way to worship al-'Aẓīm.

▪ When you see something that is being touted as great but it actually deemed reprehensible by Allah, remember to reorient your standards.

DU'A

Ya Aẓīm, let me see Your greatness in everything You have created, and to aspire to Your standards of greatness.

REFLECTIVE QUESTION

Consider the things that you consider to be great - are they in conformity or in opposition to the criteria that al-'Aẓīm has placed for greatness?

الْغَفُور

AL-GHAFŪR

THE OFT-FORGIVING

'Say, "O My servants who have gone to extremes against themselves: despair not of Allah's mercy, for indeed Allah forgives all misdeeds; indeed, He is the Oft-Forgiving, the Bestower of mercy.'
(39:53)

STORY

As human beings, it may be natural to turn away from someone who messes up constantly, especially if they make the same mistake over and over again. We look at such a person and think 'they'll never learn'. We might pity them or be frustrated with them. If their transgressions are against us, we might give them a couple of chances, but at some point, we will close the door and may even cut them off. Because we operate at this mortal level, we somehow think this mode of being applies to Allah as well. But the fact that He named Himself al-Ghafūr is to tell us precisely that He is not like that. He reminds us by this name that His door is always open, no matter how many mistakes we make. It is to make us hopeful that even if we mess up a hundred times, Allah still gives us opportunities to become better and to return to Him. Knowing this name should empower us because we know that Allah is giving us opportunities to be better. He is telling us that we do not need to get stuck in our sins and indiscretions, but rather we can break that cycle. We do not have to be defined by our mistakes because He forgives them. The process of seeking forgiveness means that we are being reflective: identifying our mistakes, recognizing that they are wrong, humbling ourselves by seeking forgiveness from Allah, and working on our development by putting in the effort to stop the sin, not return to it, and replace it with something good. Knowing al-Ghafūr guides us to this, so that we are in a constant state of self-improvement and spiritual refinement.

Al-Ghafūr is the One who forgives all sins, no matter their quantity.

- Ar-Raḥīm – The Especially Merciful (2:54)
- Al-Ḥalīm – Forbearing (3:155)
- Al-Afū – Pardonerg (58:3)
- Al-'Azīz – The Strongy (35:28)
- Ash-Shakūr – the Appreciative (35:30)

- When you feel guilty of constantly sinning and are wondering if you can ever break the cycle.
- When we are tempted to give up on people because of their constant mistakes.
- When we feel unforgiving towards others.

Ya Ghafūr, forgive all of my sins, those which I did intentionally and those which I did unintentionally, those which I remember and those which I don't.

When you committed a wrong in the past, was it easy for you to turn back to Allah? How will this change now that you know His name al-Ghafūr?

ُ ّٰ

الشَّكُور

ASH-SHAKŪR

THE MOST APPRECIATIVE

'Whoever earns a good deed, We will increase it in goodness for them. Surely Allah is All-Forgiving, Most Appreciative.' (42:23)

STORY

We often hear stories about the pious: the scholar who spends the majority of every night praying; the generous person who donated all of his or her wealth; the person who left a great legacy. These examples can be incredibly inspiring for us, but they may also cause us to question whether our small deeds – which we cannot see as even coming close to these enormous good works we hear about – even matter. But this is why Allah reminds us that He is ash-Shakūr: He appreciates, loves, and rewards all good deeds, no matter how small. Indeed, He is so appreciative that He takes into account your intention, thereby making a seemingly small deed magnificent. You could be in a bad mood or upset at something that happened to you, but you find the strength to muster up a genuine smile and kind words to a stranger or loved one. This might seem negligible, but Allah knows you did so for His sake, and He appreciates this deed by multiplying its reward. Indeed, it could be this seemingly small act that enters you into Paradise. This is the why the Prophet ﷺ not only praised those who did objectively great actions – such as the Companion Uthman who donated all of his wealth – but he encouraged those actions that are considered minor, such as smiling at people, donating even half a date in charity, and quenching the thirst of an animal. Knowing ash-Shakūr teaches us that no deed is too small, even if people see it as so, because it is beloved in the sight of Allah. In an era when people showcase their greatest achievements online, it may make us wonder what is the point in doing things that cannot match them, but knowing ash-Shakūr teaches us to focus on those deeds that Allah loves and appreciates, and not simply what is valued by people.

Ash-Shakūr is the One who accepts and appreciates all good deeds, no matter how small, and rewards generously for them.

- Al-Ḥalīm – Clement (64:17)
- Al-'Alīm – All-Knowing (4:147)
- Al-Ghafūr – The Oft-Forgiving (42:23)

- If ever you question the point of doing something good but is small, remember that Allah appreciates all deeds.
- Appreciate other people's good actions, even when they are small.
- When you feel that you aren't doing enough good in life.

Ya Shakūr, enable us to do good deeds and be sincere and consistent in them regardless of how big or small they may be.

How often do you appreciate and thank people even for their smallest efforts for you?

الْعَلِيُّ الْمُتَعَال

AL-'ALĪ
AL-MUTA'ĀL

THE MOST HIGH, THE TRANSCENDENT

*'To Him belongs whatever is in the heavens and whatever is
on the earth. And He is the Most High, the Greatest.' (42:4)*

STORY

We all have aspirations. Some of us aspire to live a good and decent life, surrounded by our loved ones. Some of us might aspire to be famous, others to leave a legacy, and others to acquire wealth. People say, 'aim for the stars', and some aspirations are regarded as 'high' and others 'low'. When our aspirations stop at this worldly life, what we are actually saying is that this world is the highest thing in our eyes. But when we know that Allah is al-'Alī al-Muta'āl, and live in light of that knowledge, we are reminded that He is the highest aspiration we can have and far transcendent above any worldly aim. He is the Most High, so our hopes and ambitions can never be greater or higher than Him. But in fact, when we fail to aspire to His pleasure, our goals are at best not lofty enough and, at worst, lowly. Aiming for His pleasure means striving to do what He loves in every circumstance: whether we are Islamic scholars, parents, students, workers, artists, doctors, philanthropists etc. It means not lowering ourselves to the standards of this world when they conflict with the standards set by the Most High. Knowing al-'Alī al-Muta'āl also means humbling ourselves. Indeed, when we are at the lowest point physically in prayer, and our foreheads touch the ground in reverence to Allah, we proclaim "Glorified is my Lord, the Most High". We remind ourselves that the way to be elevated is by humbling ourselves to Him.

Al-'Alī is the One who is elevated above everything in every meaning possible: in rank, in majesty, and in conception, and al-Muta'āl is the One who is transcendent above all His creation.

* Al-'Aẓīm – The Tremendous (2:255)
* Al-Kabīr – The Great (40:12)
* Al-Ḥakīm – Most Wise (41:51)

SITUATION

* Have high and lofty aspirations because your Lord is the Most High.
* Elevate what the Most High elevates.
* Whenever you get the urge to feel high above others, humble yourself before Him.

DU'A

Ya Alī, raise our aspirations so that the pinnacle of what we aim for is Your pleasure and Paradise.

REFLECTIVE QUESTION

Do you aspire to the pleasure of al-'Alī?

AL-KABĪR

THE GREAT, THE SUPREME

*"'What did your Lord say?' They say, 'The truth; and He is
the All-High, the Supreme.'"* (39:53)

STORY

We start the prayer with "Allāhu akbar" – Allah is the Greatest, thus both praising Him and reminding ourselves that He is greater. When we announce that, we should understand that He is truly greater than anything and everything: He is greater than our problems, He is greater than the temptations of the world, He is greater than our worries, and He is greater than what the world can offer us. In prayer, this means leaving the physical world behind – and whatever hold it has on our hearts – and turning with our whole beings to Allah. Praying five times a day helps us to internalize this meaning as we go about our daily lives. Are we facing an obstacle? Allah is greater than it, and thus we can overcome it by Him. Are we being offered worldly benefits that violate our sacred norms? Allah is greater than any perceived advantage, for He owns this world and the next. Is someone making our life difficult or wronging us? Allah is greater than they are, and can put a stop to their plans and deeds in an instant. Do we think ourselves 'great' because of what we have achieved or have been given? Allah is greater than we are. This name should thus engender both humility and strength; humility before al-Kabīr because He is far greater than we could ever be, and strength that is derived from knowing and turning to al-Kabīr in the face of hardships and obstacles, temptations and enticements.

Al-Kabīr is the One who is incomparably great. The word kabīr is used to describe something that is both big or great in size and rank; thus al-Kabīr is One whose greatness cannot be contained, and He is indeed greater in every way possible than everything other than Him.

* When you face an obstacle whether it be a person or challenge.
* When you find yourself becoming arrogant.
* When you begin the prayer with "Allāhu akbar".

Ya Kabīr, do not make anything greater for us than Yourself, Your Pleasure, Your Love and Your Commandments, and protect us from going astray.

* Al-'Alī – The Most High (40:12)
* Al-Muta'āl – Transcendent (15:9)

Describe a time when you were dealing with someone and you felt constricted and scared, how would the name al-Kabīr help you in these situations?

الحَفيظ

AL-ḤAFĪẒ

THE GUARDIAN

'God is the best guardian and the Most Merciful of the merciful.'
(12:64)

STORY

People refer to others who have helped them in times of need, are there for them in different circumstances, and protect them against others, as 'their guardian angels'. Knowing you have someone like that brings comfort and a sense of safety; you know that you have someone to rely on to protect you. Indeed, when a loved one passes away, people also claim that they feel their presence with them, and that they are watching over them and protecting them. Now, every mortal 'guardian' can fail us and, as a matter of theology, our loved ones who have passed away cannot physically do anything for us. So Allah reminds us that He is al-Ḥafīẓ - the Guardian and the Protector. Imagine that your guardian is the Most Powerful, the Most Merciful, and the Most Affectionate. Indeed, He is the One who cares for you most and wants the best for you in the final abode. Reflect on the times when you or your loved ones have been protected. Even if you are injured, or something bad happens to someone you love, this does not negate this attribute of Allah; remember that the Prophet ﷺ was also injured in battle, and companions were martyred. Hurt in our lives serves a purpose: sometimes, like in Sūrat al-Kahf, what appears to be a lack of protection is actually a shield against greater harm (when the boat of the poor people was damaged, it protected them from having it seized by the King; when the son passed away, it was because he would grow to harm his parents and others) or to guard one's Hereafter. Thus we should always turn to Him for both protection in this life and the next.

Al-Ḥafīẓ is He who preserves, safeguards, and protects all things under His care.

- When you feel a lack of protection and vulnerability.
- Observe God's limits, as Allah describes the believers as those who 'observe (ḥafiẓūn) God's limits. Give glad news to such believers.' (9:112)
- Protect the weak: just like we want al-Ḥafīẓ to protect us due to our weakness, we should protect others who need help and guardianship.

Ya Ḥafīẓ, protect our bodies and hearts from harm in this world, and protect us from the punishment in the next world.

Reflect on situations in your life where events did not pan out the way you expected them to, now think about His name Al-Ḥafīẓ and His guardianship.

الْمُقِيت

AL-MUQĪT

THE NOURISHER, THE SUSTAINER

'And Allah has always been a Sustainer for everything.'
(4:85)

STORY

This name is similar to His name ar-Razzāq but is more specific as it relates specifically to nourishment, whereas ar-Razzāq provides different forms of sustenance, some having to do with nourishment and others not. When you think of al-Muqīt, always think of those things you consider as nourishment for both your body and your soul. The nourishment of your body is in the good (healthy) and pure (from permissible and ethical means) food that you eat; and that is from al-Muqīt. Indeed, He creates all the nourishment that we need to sustain us. But we know that we are not just nourished by the food we eat, which only sustains our bodies, we are also nourished by the food that our soul needs. Allah al-Muqīt provides us that nourishment in the Qur'an, the example of the Prophet ﷺ and those who follow him, the remembrances, circles of knowledge and company of the pious, and so on. These too are from al-Muqīt in order to nourish our souls. Thus, just like we go out to get the food that we need to feed our bodies – which has been provided by al-Muqīt – we should also go out and seek the nourishment for our souls, because al-Muqīt will provide it.

MEANING

Al-Muqīt is the Nourisher and Sustainer of all His creatures, giving both materially and spiritually, and He responds to those who are desperate.

SITUATION

- Be grateful for the food that al-Muqīt has provided you, and remember not to corrupt it.
- When you feel your soul and spirituality are malnourished.
- Nourish others from what Allah has nourished you with; whether that is materially or spiritually.

DU'A

Ya Muqīt, nourish our souls with your remembrance, and nourish our bodies with sustenance that is good and pure.

REFLECTIVE QUESTION

Do you take care of the nourishment of your soul as much as the nourishment of your body?

الحَسِيب

AL-ḤASĪB

THE RECKONER, THE SUFFICIENT

'Indeed, Allah has always been a Reckoner of everything.'
(4:86)

STORY

Many of us know the phrase "Ḥasbī Allah wa ni'm al-Wakīl", which roughly translates to 'Sufficient is Allah for me, and He is the best Trustee'. We may say it daily as part of our remembrances. We might know that the Prophet Ibrahim (as) said this phrase before he was catapulted into the raging fire by his people, which Allah made cool and safe for him. We might be familiar with the name stated at the end of the phrase; 'al-Wakīl' or the Trustee. But the first part of the phrase is crucial as well. We say : 'Ḥasbī Allah', meaning that Allah is sufficient for us. He is al-Ḥasīb, who suffices anyone who relies on Him. He is enough. Knowing that Allah is al-Ḥasīb means knowing that we can turn to Him in all circumstances. It means knowing that if we have Allah, we have all we need. It means knowing that if we place our trust in Him, then He will never let us down. This does not mean that we will not be tested – the Prophets, Messengers, and the righteous were tested the most – but it means that He will be with us, helping us to confront and withstand whatever comes our way. And it is in this fact that we take comfort in. The other meaning of the name al-Ḥasīb is that He takes to account all deeds. We are reminded that, 'whoever does an atom's weight of good sees it, and whoever does an atom's weight of evil sees it.' (99:7-8) Knowing that Allah sees and takes into account all deeds, no matter how big or small, should teach us not to minimize good or bad deeds – in terms of performance of good or avoidance of evil – even if they appear to be minor. It should also give us hope that no good deed or intention is ever overlooked.

Al-Ḥasīb is the One who takes account of all deeds, and He is sufficient for anyone who truly relies on Him.

- Whenever you face difficulty, and do not know where to turn to.
- When a person has let you down and you relied too much on them.

Ya Ḥasīb, You are Sufficient for us in all matters. Ya Ḥasīb, protect us from ourselves from being more dependent on others than on You and always guide us to seek Your assistance.

When you recite the du'a 'Ḥasbī Allah wa ni'm al-Wakīl', how does that make you feel knowing that you are affirming that Allah is enough for you?

الجَليل ذو الجَلالِ والإكْرام

AL-JALĪL
DHŪ AL-JALĀL
WA AL-IKRĀM

THE MAJESTIC, THE POSSESSOR OF MAJESTY AND GENEROSITY

'And all that remains is your Lord's Countenance, the Possessor of majesty and nobility.' (55:27)

STORY

Think of the last time that you were overcome with awe. Perhaps it was when you stood in front of a mountain or valley, and you were in awe out of the majesty of the creation of Allah. Maybe it was when you witnessed the power of nature, in the form of a typhoon or hurricane. It may have been when something unexpected happened to you that humbled you to your core. These are all manifestations of Allah al-Jalīl – the Majestic - and Dhū al-Jalāl wa al-Ikrām - Possessor of Majesty and Generosity. All of these moments should cause us to prostrate in awe of al-Jalīl.

Al-Jalīl and Dhū al-Jalāl wa al-Ikrām is the One who is majestic in His essence and all His attributes are majestic; His generosity is also as befits His majesty, inspiring awe in His creation.

SITUATION
- When we look at a person or material thing with too much awe remember that Allah is the Majestic.
- When we feel that we have a lack of resources in life, remember Allah is the most Generous.

DU'A

Ya Dhū al-Jalāl wa al-Ikrām, allow us to always remember and appreciate Your possession of the heavens and the earth and Your majesty.

REFLECTIVE QUESTION

Reflect deeply about how your heart feels when it hears about the majesty of Allah, for example, through listening to the Qur'an.

MEMORIZATION LIST

Ar-Raḥmān	1	○
Ar-Raḥīm	2	○
Al-Malik	3	○
Al-Quddūs	4	○
As-Salām	5	○
Al-Mu'min	6	○
Al-Muhaymin	7	○
Al-'Azīz	8	○
Al-Jabbār	9	○
Al-Mutakabbir	10	○
Al-Khāliq	11	○
Al-Bāri'	12	○
Al-Muṣawwir	13	○
Al-Ghaffār	14	○
Al-Qahhār	15	○
Al-Wahhāb	16	○
Ar-Razzāq	17	○
Al-Fattāḥ	18	○
Al-'Alīm	19	○
Al-Qābiḍ	20	○
Al-Bāsiṭ	21	○
Al-Khāfiḍ	22	○
Ar-Rāfi'	23	○
Al-Mu'izz	24	○
Al-Mudhill	25	○
As-Samī'	26	○
Al-Baṣīr	27	○
Al-Ḥakam	28	○
Al-'Adl	29	○
Al-Laṭīf	30	○
Al-Khabīr	31	○
Al-Ḥalīm	32	○
Al-'Aẓīm	33	○
Al-Ghafūr	34	○
Ash-Shakūr	35	○
Al-'Alī	36	○
Al-Kabīr	37	○
Al-Ḥafīẓ	38	○
Al-Muqīt	39	○
Al-Ḥasīb	40	○
Al-Jalīl	41	○
Al-Karīm	42	○
Ar-Raqīb	43	○
Al-Mujīb	44	○
Al-Wāsi'	45	○
Al-Ḥakīm	46	○
Al-Wadūd	47	○
Al-Majīd	48	○
Al-Bā'ith	49	○
Ash-Shahīd	50	○
Al-Ḥaqq	51	○
Al-Wakīl	52	○
Al-Qawī	53	○
Al-Matīn	54	○
Al-Walī	55	○
Al-Ḥamīd	56	○
Al-Muḥṣī	57	○
Al-Mubdi'	58	○
Al-Mu'īd	59	○
Al-Muḥyī	60	○
Al-Mumīt	61	○
Al-Ḥayy	62	○
Al-Qayyūm	63	○
Al-Wājid	64	○
Al-Mājid	65	○
Al-Wāḥid	66	○
Al-Aḥad	67	○
Aṣ-Ṣamad	68	○
Al-Qādir	69	○
Al-Qadīr	70	○
Al-Muqtadir	71	○
Al-Muqaddim	72	○
Al-Mu'akhir	73	○
Al-Awwal	74	○
Al-Ākhir	75	○
Az-Ẓāhir	76	○
Al-Bāṭin	77	○
Al-Walī	78	○
Al-Muta'āl	79	○
Al-Barr	80	○
At-Tawwāb	81	○
Al-Muntaqim	82	○
Al-'Afuww	83	○
Ar-Ra'ūf	84	○
Mālik al-Mulk	85	○
Dhū al-Jalāl wa al-Ikrām	86	○
Al-Muqsiṭ	87	○
Al-Jāmi'	88	○
Al-Ghanī	89	○
Al-Mughnī	90	○
Al-Māni'	91	○
Aḍ-Ḍārr	92	○
An-Nāfi'	93	○
An-Nūr	94	○
Al-Hādī	95	○
Al-Badī'	96	○
Al-Bāqī	97	○
Al-Wārith	98	○
Ar-Rashīd	99	○
As-Sabūr	100	○
Allah	101	○

الكَرِيم

AL-KARĪM

THE GENEROUS, THE NOBLE

'O humanity! What has emboldened you against your Lord, the Most Generous?' (82:6)

STORY

When we encounter a generous person, we naturally feel positively towards them. A person's generous actions – they may give without being prompted, and they give more than is expected – lead us to have a good opinion of them and see them as noble. Now ponder this: a human being's generosity has constraints, because what we have is naturally limited, and we have needs ourselves. A person's generosity is not even a fraction of Allah's generosity, who named Himself al-Karīm so that we can know that no one is more generous or noble than Him. Indeed, we only need to look around us to realize that everything given to us is above and beyond. Flowers do not need to be pleasing, nor food tasty; they only need to fulfill a function. But they are beautiful. We do not need to be rewarded for worshipping Allah – He created us! – yet He rewards us for what is obligatory upon us. He even rewards our unfulfilled intentions when they are good. And for a limited time on earth – one that is mixed with joy and sorrow, pleasure and pain – He has prepared for us eternal bliss that erases any pain we might have felt in this world. He gives us without asking – ponder upon the blessings you have in your life that you did not ask for – and when we do ask, He guarantees that He will respond with what is best for us. Al-Karīm is so generous that He assures us that no matter how much we messed up, not only will He forgive, but He will give us blessings and rewards!

Al-Karīm is generous in every single meaning of the word: He is magnanimous when He gives, so much so that He exceeds all expectations and goes beyond what we can imagine, He forgives all mistakes and slip-ups, and He honors the generous and righteous among us.

- Al-Ghanī - Self-Sufficient (27:40)

SITUATION

- When you are questioning and wondering why Allah has not gifted you something, remember all of the things He has gifted you with.
- Ponder over what you have and reflect upon how over and beyond your needs they are.
- Be generous with others just as you love for Allah to be generous with you.

DU'A

Ya Karīm, never deprive us from bestowing Your blessings upon us.

REFLECTIVE QUESTION

Do you go above and beyond when you give people? Have you ever reflected on how Allah has gone above and beyond in your own life?

AR-RAQĪB

THE WATCHER, THE OBSERVER

'Indeed, Allah has always been Watchful over you.' (4:1)

STORY

Ar-Raqīb is similar to His name al-Basīr – the All-Seeing – in the sense that it tells us that He sees us. However, the connotations are different because the meaning of raqīb includes one who watches over. Allah says in the Qur'an, 'you are under Our watchful eye.' (52:48) Thus, ar-Raqīb not only sees us, but He observes and watches over us with His care. Of course, many of us know theoretically that Allah watches over us. But living with the meaning of this name means to worship Allah with ihsan (excellence), which the Prophet ﷺ described as worshipping Allah 'as though you see Him, and though you do not see Him, you know that He sees you.' (Bukhārī) Knowing ar-Raqīb is also to be reassured that He is not oblivious to what is going on, but that He is watching all events as they unfold. It is to be cognizant that our deeds are being seen in real-time by ar-Raqīb, which should help us to be more purposeful and deliberate in our behavior. It should also engender shyness and modesty as we stand before Allah.

Ar-Raqīb is the One who watches over and is observant of everything.

- When we make movements in life such as leaving home, or greeting our parents, know that the Watcher is observing you.
- Knowing that the Most Powerful and Most Merciful is watching over us should give us comfort when times are tough.

Ya Raqib, endow us with the awareness that You are watching over us in every second, and grant us comfort and vigilance with that awareness.

When you internalize that Allah is watching over you - both outwardly and inwardly - how does that change your focus and devotion?

المُجِيب

AL-MUJĪB

THE RESPONSIVE, THE ANSWERER OF PRAYERS

'My Lord is indeed Near, Responsive.' (11:61)

STORY

We all need help and assistance, and many of us go to certain people who are close to us and whom we trust for that help. We avoid going to someone we know cannot or would not help us, or someone whom we feel our request would burden. Now, who is actually the closest one to us? Who is truly the most able to help us? Who is the one who wants our ultimate benefit? Allah has given Himself the name al-Mujīb in order to assure us that He will respond. It is not simply an attribute or an action – i.e. something that He does – but rather a name i.e something that He is. He is the Responsive, the Answerer of prayers. And how amazing that He combines this name in the Qur'an with His name al-Qarīb – the Near, to let us know how intimately aware He is of all of our needs. For that reason, the Prophet ﷺ reminded us that, 'When one of you supplicates, let him be determined in the supplication and he should not say: "O Allah, give me if you will." There is none to coerce Allah.' (Bukhārī and Muslim) But if He is al-Mujīb, then why does it appear that some prayers are not answered? Ibn Aṭā'illāh said, 'If in spite of intense supplication, there is delay in the timing of the Gift, let that not be the cause for your despairing. For He has guaranteed you a response in what He chooses for you, not in what you choose for yourself, and at the time He desires, not the time you desire.' This is important to understand. Allah is al-Mujīb, meaning He will respond. However, because He is not just al-Mujīb, but He is also the Most Wise and the Most Merciful, His response to you will always be what is truly best for you, and not what you think is best for you. So He never does not respond, and because He is also the Most Generous, He will never turn you away with nothing, and will give you that which is actually good for you, even though you did not ask for it. Moreover, knowing that He is the Pure should remind us that our source of income should be pure because that may block a response to our supplication.

Al-Mujīb is the One who responds to the caller when He calls on Him, and gives His servants what is best for them.

- Al-Qarīb – The Near (11:61)

SITUATION

- When you feel your du'as are not being answered in a way that you are expecting them to be, know that al-Mujīb is also the One who is closest to you and the Most Wise, so His response is what is actually best for this life and the next.
- When you perceive a delay in the response, have certainty that the answer is guaranteed, and do not give up hope.

DU'A

Ya Mujīb, You are closer to us than our jugular vein and You hear every plea of Your servant. Ya Mujīb, grant us the best response to our dua's.

REFLECTIVE QUESTION

How are your expectations set when you make du'a to Allah? How might you adjust your expectations to be more in line with His name al-Mujīb?

الوَاسِع

AL-WĀSI'

THE VAST, THE ALL-EMBRACING

'Indeed, Allah is All-Embracing, All-Knowing.' (2:115)

STORY

Allah mentions His name al-Wāsi' or the attribute of vastness in the Qur'an with four other attributes: His forgiveness (53:32); His mercy (7:156); His wisdom (4:130); and His knowledge (20:98). This has many implications for us. When we commit too many mistakes and cannot forgive ourselves, Allah's vast forgiveness applies to us. When we are treated with harshness by the closest people to us, we know that we can turn to al-Wāsi', whose mercy knows no bounds. It means that when we feel out of place, Allah's vastness can encompass us. And when we feel as though we do not fit in, Allah is the All-Embracing. His name al-Wāsi' also brings hope from another dimension. While we all have the same personal obligations and must abide by the same prohibitions, outside of that, there are so many ways to Allah – He is the Vast. He is not limited by what people perceive to be the only way to be religious, as long as it falls within the permissible. You can be beloved to Allah al-Wāsi' through your ethical work, your conscious parenting, your kindness to others, your educational writing, or your cooking for others. All of these – and more! – are ways to Allah.

Al-Wāsi' is the Vast and the All-Embracing, meaning there is no end to His wisdom or mercy or knowledge, and because He is vast, His mercy encompasses you.

- Al-'Alīm – the All-Knowing (3:73)
- Al-Ḥakīm – Most Wise (4:130)

SITUATION

- When you feel out of place.
- When you are up against the impossible.
- When you struggle, know that Allah is far too vast to reject you when you are sincerely trying for His sake.

DU'A

Ya Wāsi', embrace me with Your all-encompassing mercy.

REFLECTIVE QUESTION

Think of a moment when you felt the absolute vastness of Allah's support in your life, when He made something impossible in your eyes, become possible.

الْحَكِيم

AL-ḤAKĪM

'Allah thus clarifies His signs for you. For Allah is All-Knowing, All-Wise.' (24:59)

STORY

A story is narrated about a king who had an advisor who constantly responded to what appeared to be bad with 'perhaps there is good in it.' This irritated the king, but he never reacted. On an excursion to a nearby forest, the king was injured and lost his finger. The advisor again said, 'perhaps there is good in it.' This time the king could not hold himself back; what good could there be in him losing his finger?! So he threw his advisor in prison for his perceived insolence. The advisor again said, 'perhaps there is good in it.' The king went back to the forest alone, and was ambushed by a tribe. They tied him up and wanted to sacrifice him to their gods. Just before they sacrificed him at the altar, one of the elders screamed at them to stop. He had noticed that the king had a missing finger. They quickly untied him and let him go; they could not dedicate a defective sacrifice to their gods. The king, visibly shaken, returned back to the prison where he had thrown his advisor. He related the story to his advisor, who simply smiled. Before releasing him, he asked, 'We now know the good that came as a result of losing my finger, but what was good in you being put in prison?' The advisor said, 'Your majesty, had I not been put in prison, I would have been with you, and they would have then sacrificed me at the altar!' While this is an endearing story, it actually leads to Allah's name al-Ḥakīm. Allah is the Most Wise, meaning that all His actions emanate from this flawless wisdom, and all of the rules prescribed for us have wisdom ingrained in them. There is wisdom in every decree, whether it appears to be good or bad. Thus, when things occur that are outside of our control, we should know that there is wisdom in it that may become apparent later on. Even if it does not become apparent in this life, we will see God's wisdom in the Hereafter.

Al-Ḥakīm is the One who is the most wise, and who only decrees things out of His wisdom.

- Al-'Azīz - Almighty (64:18)
- Al-'Alīm - All-Knowing (6:139)
- Al-'Alī - Most High (42:51)
- Al-Khabīr - All-Aware (6:18)
- Al-Ḥamīd - Praiseworthy (41:42)

SITUATION

- When things do not go as you had wanted or expected, learn from the situation, and know that there is wisdom in it.
- Knowledge alone cannot help us, only in how we employ our knowledge. Thus, learn from this name of Allah by asking for and cultivating wisdom in your actions.

DU'A

Ya Ḥakīm, grant us wisdom when dealing with our affairs, and enable us to always have a good opinion of You when things do not go the way we wanted them to.

REFLECTIVE QUESTION

What events in your life appeared to be bad, but you later discovered contained wisdom or benefit in them?

الوَدُود

AL-WADŪD

THE LOVING, THE AFFECTIONATE

'And ask forgiveness of your Lord and then repent to Him.
Indeed, my Lord is Merciful and Affectionate.' (11:90)

STORY

One of the strongest and most fulfilling emotions that one can experience is love, particularly feeling loved. Allah knows this about us – indeed, He placed this in us – and thus He tells us that He is the Most Loving and Affectionate; He is al-Wadūd. And what does love mean? It means care, affection, and wanting the best for the beloved. Look at your life: you might have difficulty, but you have many blessings as well. Even the difficulties you went through contained blessings, and taught you things you otherwise would not have known. Indeed, sometimes, we only get to know who truly loves us when we are in hardship; it is easy to be around fair-weathered friends, or people who accompany us when we are at our best. But going through hardship means that we turn to those whom we love and those whom we know love us. Knowing al-Wadūd means knowing that you can go to Him when you feel down and alone. It means going back to Him when we have messed up. It means reciting the Qur'an knowing that the words are from al-Wadūd. It means praying with a heart filled with love knowing you are standing before al-Wadūd. It means looking at the troubles in your life from this perspective: there must be love and affection in them. And know that you would not be reading these words if He did not want you to know this attribute. Thus, if you want to be a recipient of al-Wadūd's special love, do the things that bring about His love: do good, be God-conscious, be of those who constantly return to Allah and constantly purify themselves.

Al-Wadūd is the Most Loving and Affectionate, who manifests His love to His creation.

- Al-Ghafūr – Oft-Forgiving (85:14)
- Ar-Rahīm – Merciful (11:90)

- If ever you feel unworthy of love because of how people have made you feel.
- Always act and respond from a place of love, and see how that changes your interactions with people.

Ya Wadūd, grant us Your love, the love of people who love You, and love for deeds that bring us closer to Your love.

Have you ever considered that Allah loves you? How does that make you feel knowing you have a Lord who not only loves you, but bestows that love and affection upon you?

'He is indeed Praiseworthy, Glorious.' (11:73)

STORY

Many people seek majd – glory – through different means. Without guidance, people can think that glory is in showing might, or in receiving attention and being praised. But if one were to truly reflect, is this really glory? Is exerting power unjustly glorious? Is fame based on having 30 million Instagram followers actually magnificent? Allah reminds us through these names that there can never be true glory in what He dislikes; He is al-Majīd and al-Mājid, who truly possesses glory. These names tell us that Allah is noble in His essence, beautiful in His actions, and bountiful in His giving. In prayer, when we say the ṣalawāt upon the Prophet ﷺ, we also say to Allah, "You are al-Ḥamīd (the Praiseworthy) al-Majīd." We are reminding ourselves of the glory of God, of how magnificent all of His attributes and actions are. Thus, when we see people seek glory through improper means or we ourselves are absorbed by the idea, we should turn to the truly Glorious and Magnificent.

Al-Majīd and al-Mājid are both from the same root mīm-jīm-dāl, which means glory. These names mean that Allah in His essence and attributes is Glorious and Magnificent.

- Al-Ḥamīd – Praiseworthy (11:73)

SITUATION

- Never seek glory that is based on worldly standards; remember that Allah is al-Majīd and al-Mājid, and true glory is in closeness to Him.
- Never glorify or praise that which Allah does not love; we tend to be impressed by those who have achieved splendor in this world even though their actions are disliked by Allah.

DU'A

Ya Majīd, Ya Mājid, enable us to recognize Your glory in the universe.

REFLECTIVE QUESTION

How would you define glory? How does your definition compare to what is truly glorified by Allah?

البَاعِث

AL-BĀ'ITH

THE RAISER, THE RESURRECTOR

'And because the Hour is indeed coming—there is no doubt about it—and because indeed Allah resurrects those in the graves.' (22:7)

STORY

It is easy to be distracted by the world and the events that happen around us. But if we were to take a step back, we might just realize that the majority of those things that are vying for our attention are mere diversions from the path we are supposed to be on: the path to Allah. Knowing al-Bā'ith is to have certainty that we will be raised again and, thus, what we do and what we allow to take our attention matter. Knowing we will ultimately be resurrected should jolt us into waking up from heedlessness and infuse purpose into our lives. We can start by asking ourselves: in what state would I like to be raised up again? Indeed, we are told that each person will be resurrected upon what he or she died upon. Do we want to be resurrected scrolling through our social media channels? Or do we want to be resurrected reciting the Qur'an, or helping others? Moreover, this should cause us to reflect on our deeds and rectify them so that when we are raised again, we have already sought forgiveness for the bad that we have done. Furthermore, al-Bā'ith is also the one who sent us a Messenger as a mercy. The Prophet Muhammad ﷺ does not speak from his own desires, and thus we learn from him how to live a purposeful and God-conscious life.

Al-Bā'ith is He who raises and sends, and thus He raises up the dead, and sends Messengers to teach His creation.

- When you find yourself consumed by the world, remember that you will be resurrected.

Ya Bā'ith, resurrect me upon the best state and the state most pleasing to you.

Upon what state would you like to be resurrected? Are you living your life in conformity with how you would like to be resurrected?

الشَّهِيد

ASH-SHAHĪD

THE WITNESS

'Say, "What thing is more solemn in testimony?" Say, "Allah is Witness between you and me".' (6:19)

STORY

Sometimes, people are called to be witnesses for specific events. These witnesses record everything, ensure that things are going smoothly, and document every discrepancy. They may not say anything in the moment, but you know that everything that is happening is being written down, and will be revealed later. Understanding this about the act of witnessing helps us to understand Allah ash-Shahīd, the ultimate Witness, who observes everything that happens. He is witness to every single event, recording every detail and nuance. But Allah is not just the Witness — we should always understand His names and attributes holistically — but He is also the Judge. Thus, when we see injustice in the world, we should know that Allah is not oblivious to anything, He is a witness to it, and He will judge accordingly on the Day of Judgment. The Qur'an tells us about the people of the trench, who were persecuted and then massacred for their beliefs, and that their persecutors' 'only grievance against them was their faith in God, the Mighty, the Praiseworthy, to whom all control over the heavens and earth belongs: God is witness over all thing.' (85:8-9). Allah was not unaware of what was happening: He is Witness to the injustice. On the Day of Judgment, those who committed injustice will face what they did and will not be able to deny it because Allah was there, witnessing it all. As for His righteous servants, they will be given Paradise for what they endured. But this name is not simply relevant to the injustice we see around us. Knowing ash-Shahīd means knowing that He is a witness to the happenings in our own lives, and thus we should ask ourselves: am I happy for Allah to witness this? Am I ok with this being laid bare on the Day of Judgment?

Ash-Shahīd witnesses everything that occurs, and is the ultimate Witness on the Day of Judgment.

* When you feel frustrated over injustice, know that Allah is witnessing everything, and no one will escape His justice.
* When you do something, ask yourself whether you are happy for Allah to witness it.

Ya Shahīd, make us witnesses to the truth and allow us to carry out our deeds knowing you are the ultimate Witness.

Are you happy with your deeds being witnessed by Allah? What would you change?

الْحَقّ

AL - ḤAQQ

THE REAL, THE TRUTH

'That is because Allah is the Truth, and because what they call upon apart from Him is falsehood.' (31:30)

STORY

What is truth? While the answer might be self-evident to some – it is something in which there is no doubt, that corresponds with reality or the actual state of affairs – in other quarters, the idea of truth is being chipped away at. We are all familiar with the notions of 'fake news' and 'alternative facts'. People live in their own echo chambers and only listen to things that affirm their worldview. The idea of truth existing is replaced by the idea that everything is relative, and everyone can have their own narrative about the truth. Absorbing this idea makes truth negotiable, and that everyone can have their own truth. While many things are relative, and personal narratives and experiences are important, there are also absolute truths. Allah reminds us that He is the Truth, the Real – He is al-Ḥaqq. What this means is that His Words (the Qur'an) are also truth; His Promise is truth and our meeting with Him is truth; Paradise and Hell are both truth, and the Day of Judgment is truth. Because He is the Truth and the Real, then we can rely on Him. We can rely on His words to know the reality of this world and the Hereafter, and thus we can be and act accordingly. It also means that we can turn to Him as our compass in this life. His is the true standard, the objective and constant truth, and everything that comes from Him leads to the truth.

Al-Ḥaqq is the Truth; meaning He is truth in and of Himself and His promise is true.

- Al-Malik – Sovereign (20:114)

SITUATION

- As servants of al-Ḥaqq, we should advocate for and live by the principles of truth.
- In this age of fake news, we should heed the warning of the Prophet ﷺ that, 'It is an evil mount for a man to rely upon what others merely assert.' (Abū Dāwūd).

DU'A

Ya Ḥaqq, enable us to recognize truth as truth and strengthen us to be firm upon it, and enable us to recognize falsehood as falsehood and help us to avoid it.

REFLECTIVE QUESTION

Ask yourself: how can I stay firm upon the truth? Do I only listen to things that affirm my view?

الوَكِيل

AL-WAKĪL

THE TRUSTEE, THE DISPOSER OF AFFAIRS

'Those to whom the people said, "The people have assembled against you, so fear them." But this only increased them in faith, and they said, "Allah is sufficient for us, and what an excellent Trustee."' (3:173)

STORY

Trust is important in any relationship. The closer we are to someone, the more we trust them. But the meaning of trust is more vast than knowing that someone will be there for you when you need them or that they will not let you down. You may not trust even the closest person to you to do something that requires a skill they do not have, no matter how much they love you and want to help you. Moreover, even with those we say we trust, part of that trust is knowing in what situation or with what things we do not trust them with. For example, a married person might not trust their spouse to remember to pick up the children from school. This might be something minor, of course, but it still tells us that we accept a lack of trust in our relationships for certain matters because we are human beings who have flaws. Yet, Allah not only tells us that He is al-Wakīl, but He invites us to 'take Him as a Trustee.' (73:9). Allah is telling us that we can place our trust in Him and He will never let us down. When you trust someone, you also trust in their wisdom to do what is best. So trust in Allah does not necessarily mean that things will always go our way, but rather that our hearts can be at ease because we know we have Him to take care of our affairs. What is required of us is to work with the means that He has provided for us, and leave the rest to Him. Once we do that, what transpires in this world will be best for us in this life and, more importantly, the next.

Al-Wakīl is the One who takes care of those who rely upon Him.

- When people have let you down and you have over-relied on them.
- A lack of means should not result in a lack of trust; rather, our trust should remain the same because our lack of means pushes us to rely on Him more rather than the means.
- We should be reliable people as servants of al-Wakīl, and not let others down.

Ya Wakīl, take care of my affairs and grant me full trust in You.

Allah is the Judge, the Witness, the Truth and the Trustee, how do these names collectively relate to you?

AL-QAWĪ

THE STRONG

'Allah has prescribed: "I will most surely overcome, I and My messengers." Indeed, Allah is Strong, Almighty.' (58:21)

STORY

We all know strength when we see it, whether it is internal or external. In the myth of Achilles, he was made strong and invulnerable, and was able to win many battles. However, his sole weakness was in his heel, and he eventually died of a wound to it. While this is, of course, a myth, it tells us something about mortal strength: everyone has weaknesses, no matter how strong and invincible they appear to be. Thus, when Allah tells us that He is al-Qawī, He is not simply telling us that He is the Strong; rather He is telling us that His strength is overpowering and impenetrable. Consequently, no one should be arrogant because of how seemingly strong they are and use that strength to hurt other people, because al-Qawī is stronger. Rather, a strong person seeks strength with al-Qawī and uses his or her strength in the service of the vulnerable, and recognizes his or her weakness before Allah.

Al-Qawī is the One who is the Most Strong, who never experiences weakness.

- When you feel weak, seek strength with al-Qawī.
- Cultivate strength for His sake, so that you are not overpowered by others.

- Al-'Azīz – The Almighty (42:19)

Ya Qawī, strengthen my heart with faith, and give me strength to be able to help others and overcome hardship.

Reflect on times in your life when you feel weakened, what caused it? How can you rely on al-Qawī to strengthen you during those times?

AL-MATĪN

THE ALL-FIRM

'Allah is the All-Providing, the Possessor of power, the All-Firm.'
(51:58)

STORY

Often we are pulled in different directions. Family obligations, cultural expectations, and worldly temptations affect our adherence to our faith and principles. Sometimes those we used to look up to falter, and this puts us on shaky ground as well. But the nature of this world is unstable. If we try to hold on to anything of this world for support, we are only as steadfast as our support is – and this world is unreliable. And thus Allah tells us that He is al-Matīn – He is the One who is completely unshakeable, never wavering, resolutely firm. This is a name to remember whenever we feel that our resolve is shaky, and we want to give up or give in to worldly enticements. We also turn to Him when our lives feel unstable - He is al-Matīn and can make us firm upon our path. Moreover, Allah also informs us: 'I will give them time. Indeed, My plan is firm (matīn).' (7:183) This is to reassure us that no one will escape the plan of God, no matter how untouchable they might seem in this world, and even if it seems that they have gained in the short-term. Indeed, when the world around the Prophet ﷺ was uncertain – when people were plotting against him, when they were enticing him to give up on the fundamentals – he held onto al-Matīn, and never wavered in his commitment. He knew what he had to remain firm upon, and what he could compromise, but in all circumstances, he sought his strength from Allah al-Matīn.

Al-Matīn is the One who is firm in strength, who is completely
unshakeable.

- Ar-Razzāq – All-Providing (51:58)
- Al-Qawī – The Strong (51:58)

- When you find yourself wavering in your faith or your principles, hold on to al-Matīn.
- When life feels unstable and unpredictable.

Ya Matīn, make me firm upon the path to You, and grant me stability in faith.

How do you deal with a situation where you feel your faith and/or principles might get compromised?

'Allah is the Ultimate Guardian of those who have attained faith; He brings them out of the darkness(es) into the light.'
(2:257)

STORY

In our personal lives, we turn to those who are close to us to guard us and protect us when we need help. In Arabic, the name of the guardian of a child is 'walī amr', literally the one who takes care of the affairs of his or her dependent. If we take a step back, we should come to the realization that we are all dependents. When Allah tells us that He is al-Walī, He is telling us that He is our Guardian and our Patron, and indeed He takes care of our affairs. Because He is al-Walī, He rules over and governs our affairs with His protection. This is for every single believer. Yet, those who desire closeness to Allah, and turn to Him fully, desiring only Him, receive special protection and friendship. God says in the Qur'an: 'Wrongdoers only have each other to protect them; the righteous have God Himself as their protector (walī).' (45:19) If we want to know the way to this closeness and protection, Allah tells us Himself: 'Whosoever acts with enmity towards a closer servant of Mine (Walī), I will indeed declare war against him. Nothing endears My servant to Me than doing what I have made obligatory upon him to do. And My servant continues to draw nearer to Me with the supererogatory (nawāfil) so that I shall love him. When I love him, I shall be his hearing with which he shall hear, his sight with which he shall see, his hands with which he shall hold, and his feet with which he shall walk. And if he asks (something) of Me, I shall surely give it to him, and if he takes refuge in Me, I shall certainly grant him it.' [Bukhārī]

Al-Walī is the ally, protector and caretaker of His friends and those who believe in Him sincerely, and al-Walī the Ruler who takes charge of His creation and governs them.

- Al-Ḥamīd – Praiseworthy (42:28)
- An-Naṣīr – The Supporter (2:107)

- When you feel distant from Allah.
- When you feel alone and you believe you have no-one around you.
- When you feel that no-one is watching over you and looking after you.

Ya Walī, take care of my affairs, and make me of those who are Your special awliyā.

Reflect on the relationship you have with Allah, how can you draw closer to Him through what He loves?

الْحَمِيد

AL-ḤAMĪD

THE PRAISEWORTHY

'And they were guided to the best of words, and they were guided to the path of the Praiseworthy.' (22:24)

STORY

Muslims say the phrase 'al-ḥamdu lillāh' often. We say it when we wish to recognize God's blessings upon us and when something good happens to us. We also say this phrase when something seemingly bad happens, in order to remind ourselves that praise is due to Him in all situations ('al-ḥamdu lillah 'alā kulli ḥāl'). When we say 'al-ḥamdu lillāh' because of something good that we have received, we are praising and thanking Him because of His actions towards us. But the word ḥamd is praise and gratitude not simply for overt favors and actions, but for the inherent qualities of the praiseworthy. Allah reminds us that He is al-Ḥamīd because He is not simply praiseworthy for His favors upon us, but for who He is in His essence and attributes. This is part of the reason why we repeat in every prayer: 'All Praise is due to God, the Lord of the Worlds.' (1:2) Thus we are taught to not solely be attached to His giving of blessings, but to Him as our Lord. We are reminded of His inherent, beautiful attributes, and thus we praise Him in all circumstances, whether good or seemingly bad, because He is Allah al-Ḥamīd.

Al-Ḥamīd is One who is worthy of all praise in His essence, attributes, and actions.

- Al-Walī – Guardian (42:28)
- Al-Majīd – Glorious (11:73)
- Al-Ḥakīm - Most Wise (41:42)
- Al-Ghanī – Self-Sufficient (2:267)
- Al-'Azīz – The Almighty (14:1)

SITUATION

- Do not make your relationship with Allah dependent solely on the blessings you receive from Him, but rather reflect on all His wonderful attributes so that you can truly realize that He is al-Ḥamīd.
- When you are questioning an outcome in life, when you were expecting a good outcome but it turned out bad, remember al-Ḥamīd.

DU'A

Ya Ḥamīd, enable us to praise and thank you as you should be praised and thanked.

REFLECTIVE QUESTION

What does the word al-ḥamdu lillah mean to you now that you know it is more vast than simply thanks?

المُحْصِي

AL-MUḤṢĪ

THE KNOWER OF EACH SEPARATE THING, THE ENUMERATOR

'He has enumerated them and counted them precisely.' (19:94)

STORY

This attribute of Allah is mentioned most frequently with regards to Allah knowing the deeds of His creation, in the context of their return to Him. Thus, one of the reasons Allah reveals this name to us is in order to make us aware that He knows all of our deeds in their nuances and their details, both their outer dimension and inner dimension, and all of it will be in 'an evident archive' (36:12). No detail will be overlooked, and 'He knows the treacherous look of the eyes and whatever the chests hide.' (40:19) Thus, knowing al-Muḥṣī means paying attention to our actions and deeds that we will face on the Day of Judgment, particularly the ones we feel that we can hide from people. Knowing Allah al-Muḥṣī means knowing that He knows all, and we will be asked about those things on the Day of Judgment. It also means wanting our good deeds to be the best that they can be. Just like we perfect a report we are submitting or ensure that a dish we are presenting to guests is both delicious and beautiful, we should want our deeds to be as beautiful as possible. Of course, the wider meaning of this name is that 'not a leaf falls but He knows it, nor a single grain in the darkness(es) of earth, nor is there anything wet or dry but is in an evident record.' (6:59) We should feel in awe of al-Muḥṣī, that nothing escapes His knowledge, and this should also cause us to feel grateful. Why? Because despite knowing everything, He is not quick to punish, but rather gives us opportunities to return to Him. Despite knowing our shortcomings, He rewards us with an eternal Paradise for the few good deeds we are able to do.

Al-Muḥṣī knows and understands the minute details of everything in existence, and His knowledge of them is not limited to knowing their number, but their inner and outer details.

- In the hadith of the Prophet ﷺ where he informs us that Allah has 99 names, and whoever 'aḥṣāhā' – from the same root of Allah's name al-Muḥṣī – will enter Paradise, the use of this word tells us that the idea is not simply to memorize the names, but to understand them, and to understand them deeply, thinking about how Allah manifests them in our lives.
- Inculcate this attribute in yourself by enumerating your mistakes so that you can fix them, and thinking about how many days you have left in this world so that you can do more good in them.

Ya Muḥṣī, You have enumerated all of my deeds, what I am conscious of and what I am not conscious of, so forgive me for the mistakes I know and the mistakes I do not know.

Think of a time when you knowingly or unknowingly were making mistakes and committing sin, yet Allah still gave you an opportunity to return to Him.

الْمُبْدِئُ الْمُعِيدُ

AL-MUBDI'
AL-MU'ĪD

THE BEGINNER, THE RESTORER

'He is certainly the One Who originates and resurrects'
(85:13)

STORY

Al-Mubdi' al-Mu'īd are names of Allah that have multiple dimensions. On the one hand, Allah tells us that He is al-Mubdi' – He is the Beginner, the One who started and began creation. Many people do not have a problem believing in a higher power that initiated creation. However, Allah adds that He is al-Mu'īd – the Restorer. It is this latter part that more people have an issue with. People today ask the same question that those before them asked 'Can it be that when we have become bones and fragments we will really be resurrected as a new creation?' (17:49). And Allah answers, 'Have they not seen that Allah, Who created the heavens and the earth, is able to create the likes of them?' (17:99) Since Allah initiated something – something that did not even exist before – surely it is even easier for Him to restore it. And thus these names come together to alert us to the fact that we will indeed be restored, and so we should pay attention to how we want to be resurrected in the Hereafter. But these names are also general. This means something beautiful, something that can give us hope: If we feel like our hearts have strayed, and we are not as good or righteous as we were previously, or we cannot taste the sweetness of faith anymore or as we used to: Allah is al-Mubdi' al-Mu'īd. Just like He is the One that enabled you to be righteous and to taste the sweetness of faith to begin with, He can bring you back. He can restore and not only restore, but make you even better than you once were. The Prophet ﷺ reminded us that, "Faith wears out in your heart as clothes wear out, so ask Allah to renew the faith in your hearts." (Tabarani) These names teach us not to give up on ourselves, but rather to turn to Him to restore the faith in our hearts.

MEANING

Al-Mubdi' al-Mu'īd is the One who initiated creation and the One who can and will restore them.

SITUATION

- When you feel that you are far from Allah, or not as committed as you once were, ask al-Mubdi' al-Mu'īd to restore faith in your heart.
- Whenever you act, have a long-term vision that includes the Hereafter, because you know that you will be resurrected.

DU'A

Ya Mubdi' Ya Mu'īd, restore our hearts to You and fill them with love for You, just like You are the One who initiated that love to begin with.

REFLECTIVE QUESTION

When your practice or faith wavers, do you lose hope and give up? What will you do now knowing that Allah can restore your faith?

'He gives life and causes death, and to Him you are returned.'
(10:56)

STORY

Many people have a difficult time with death. We view death as the end – in one sense it is because it is the end of our time on this earth – and when it comes to the death of our loved ones, it is a seemingly permanent separation that leaves a hole in our lives and our hearts. Yet both – life and death – are creations of Allah. Allah tells us that He is 'the One Who created death and life to test you as to which of you is better in conduct,' (67:2). Life and death both have their purpose: Do we do the best that we can with the life that we are given? Do we actively work to leave something good for when we die? Indeed, since we believe in the next life, death is not really the end. The Prophet ﷺ advised us to think of death frequently, in order that we are reminded of why we are here and live accordingly. Moreover, knowing that Allah is al-Mumīt helps us to reconcile with death now; as Allah told the Prophet ﷺ 'You will certainly die, and they will certainly die,' (39:30). We are reminded to 'worship your Lord until there comes to you the certainty (death),' (Qur'an, 15:99). Knowing al-Mumīt is to not be bitter or resentful over the ostensibly untimely death of a loved one, but to realize that 'to Allah we belong, and indeed to Him we are returning,' (2:156). It is to know that we will be brought to life again, and can be reunited with our loved ones, if we are mindful to do good with and for them. Moreover, knowing that Allah is al-Muḥyī – the Giver of Life – should give us hope: when we feel that our hearts are numb, He can bring them back to life.

Al-Muḥyī al-Mumīt is the One who gives life and death, and the One who can bring life out of the dead.

- When you or someone you know has a child or someone you know passes away.
- When your heart feels dead or numb, know that Allah can give life to your heart.

Ya Muḥyī Ya Mumīt, grant us life in obedience to You, and do not take our souls unless You are pleased with us.

How is your relationship with death altered when you reflect on the fact that it is Allah who gives life and death?

AL-ḤAYY

'He is the Living One; there is no god except He, so call upon Him, devoting religion to Him. All praise be to Allah, Lord of all realms.' (40:65)

STORY

Everything in this world is temporary and dependent. Everything has a beginning and an end. Therefore, nothing in this world is truly stable or reliable. Yet Allah tells us that He is al-Ḥayy – the Ever-Living who never dies – indeed His existence is outside of the realms of life and death, which are His creations. So what does it mean for us to know that He is al-Ḥayy? Two things: 'He is the Living One; there is no god except He, so call upon Him,' (40:65) and 'place your trust in the Ever-Living One Who never dies, and exalt Him with praise,' (25:58). Knowing that He is al-Ḥayy is to know that everything is reliant on Him, so why should we call upon or ask or praise what is essentially a dependent? We should go straight to the Source of Life, rather than those things that derive life from Him. Moreover, everything in this world will leave or end or die. Not al-Ḥayy – knowing this is to know that He is always with us, in life and in death, and so our closest relationship should be with the One who is there when nothing was ever there, and when nothing will be there.

Al-Ḥayy is the Ever-Living and the Source of life itself.

Al-Qayyūm – Self-Subsisting (2:255)

- Cultivate a relationship with the One who you know will always be there, because He is al-Ḥayy.
- Recognize that life is from Him, and so praise Him for the life He has given you, and try to live as righteously as you can
- Rely on Him because He is the only One who will never let you down.

Ya Ḥayy, grant us a life in obedience to You.

Reflect on your goals in life, how much emphasis have you placed on relying upon Allah to make them a reality?

القَيُّوم

AL-QAYYŪM

THE SELF-SUBSISTING, THE ALL-SUSTAINING

'Allah—there is no god but He, the Living, the All-Sustaining.' (3:2)

STORY

Al-Qayyūm is, in every second, sustaining this world. The Prophet ﷺ advised his daughter, Fatimah, to say in the morning and in the evening: 'Yā Ḥayyu yā Qayyūm, by Your mercy I seek help; rectify for me all of my affairs and do not leave me to depend on myself, even for the blink of an eye.' [Ḥakim] When we say these words, we are reminding ourselves that everything on this earth is being sustained by Him, thus we seek the mercy of the Sustainer (al-Qayyūm) to rectify our affairs. Anything that we try to do ourselves can fall short, but when we turn to the One who sustains everything, we know that He can set right all of our affairs. We are asking for His care because His care is perfect.

Al-Qayyūm is the One by whom all things are eternally managed aright.

- Al-Ḥayy – The Ever-Living (2:255)

SITUATION

- When you feel lost or at a crossroads in life on what you should do.
- When all of your affairs/goals/activities are not going according to plan.

DU'A

Ya Ḥayy Ya Qayyūm, by Your mercy I seek help; rectify for me all of my affairs and do not leave me to depend on myself, even for the blink of an eye.

REFLECTIVE QUESTION

Reflect on how it would be if the smallest task of blinking an eye is left completely upon us to do without Allah's assistance. What does this teach you about your relationship with al-Qayyūm?

AL-WĀJID

THE ALL-PERCEIVING, THE RESOURCEFUL

'Did He not find you as an orphan then sheltered you? Did He not find you unguided then guided you? And did He not find you needy then satisfied your needs?' (93:6-8)

STORY

After the Prophet ﷺ started to call people to Islam in Makkah, revelation stopped for a period of time. The idolaters mocked him, saying 'the Lord of Muhammad abandoned him'. In response, Allah revealed Sūrat aḍ-Ḍuḥā, where He not only reassured the Prophet ﷺ that He had not abandoned him, but He reminded him that He was always with him, even before he received revelation! The Prophet ﷺ was an orphan, but he was always sheltered. He was searching for guidance, and so Allah guided Him. He had different needs, and Allah satisfied them. The word used in the verses is 'wajada', from the same root as His name al-Wājid. Thus, this tells us that al-Wājid has everything to take care of our needs, that He is aware of our different states, and that He brings to us what we need, even when we do not realize it. Thus, think back on your life: perhaps you were alone, and Allah brought you a friend. Perhaps you were looking for a job, and Allah sufficed you with what you needed until you were able to find employment. Maybe you were lost, and Allah brought faith to your heart. These are all manifestations of His name al-Wājid.

Al-Wājid has many meanings, including He who perceives and possesses everything, and who lacks nothing.

- Reflect upon the times when you were in need, and al-Wājid provided for you relief. It could be in the most subtle of ways but it still comforted you at the time.
- Remember that in all situations we are in need of Him because He possesses everything and is intimately aware of all our needs, and therefore we should turn to Him and ask Him.

Ya Wājid, shelter us from the struggles we do not even know about yet and the ones we do know.

What were the moments in your life that you felt like al-Wājid brought you exactly what you needed?

الوَاحِدُ الأَحَد

AL-WĀḤID
AL-AḤAD

THE ONE, THE UNIQUE

'Say, "He is Allah, the Uniquely One."' (112:1)

STORY

Most Muslims know the famous story of the Companion Bilāl, who was enslaved, and then accepted Islam. He was tortured for his belief, and in response, He only said 'Aḥad' in the face of his tormentors, affirming the oneness of Allah and negating the existence of any other deity or equal beside Him. This fundamental belief gave Bilāl the strength to remain steadfast. When we truly internalize the meaning of Allah being al-Wāḥid al-Aḥad, we will come to the realization that nothing comes close to Him in His strength or His power; so why would we fear anything other than Him? When we comprehend these meanings, we realize that He is the only Lord, and everyone else is subject to His will, so why would we go to anyone else for our needs? When we truly feel the effect of these names, we realize that He should be One in our hearts. He created us, He continues to give us, and He bestows incomparable mercy upon us. We are told in the Qur'an, 'Say, "What is revealed to me is that your God is one (wāḥid) God — will you submit to Him?"' (21:108) Part of this submission is not to make anything of this world equal to Him in our hearts. There should be no false idols, not simply the ones made out of wood and stone, but the false idols of status, wealth, or fame.

Allah al-Wāḥid al-Aḥad is One: He is the only deity, the only One worthy of worship, He is One and Unique in His essence and attributes, and nothing is similar to Him.

- Al-Qahhār – The Dominant (13:16)
- Aṣ-Ṣamad – The Eternal Refuge (6:54)

- When you find yourself being consumed by worldly enticements.
- Always remind yourself Allah is One, Unique, and nothing is equal to Him. Thus, reflect on the state of your heart: have you made anything equal to Him?
- When reciting Sūrat al-Ikhlāṣ, which is described as being a third of the Qur'an, and is the only chapter to mention His name al-Aḥad.

Ya Wāḥid, there is none worthy of worship except You Who has no partners, for You is the Dominion and for You is all the praise, in Your hand is all good and You are able to do all things.

Reflect and try to find out if there is anything in your life that you have unintentionally made equal to Allah.

AṢ-ṢAMAD

THE ETERNAL REFUGE

'Allah, the Eternal Refuge,' *(112:2)*

STORY

When a structure is described as 'ṣamad', it means that it is sturdy, with no holes in it. Indeed, the word 'ṣumūd' is steadfastness, and when you say that someone is 'ṣāmid' it means that he or she is firm upon their principles or belief, unmoving. Now, imagine you were on a ship at sea and, suddenly, there is a furious storm. The waves become violent, bashing the ship, as everything starts to fall apart. What would you hold on to? The broken wood from the ship? It would likely not help you. What about the lifeboat? If the storm was able to destroy a huge ship, there would be no chance for a flimsy lifeboat. Now imagine you suddenly see a structure that is sturdy, even as it is being thrashed by the waves. Even with the powerful storm, there is no breakage in this structure. You would swim to this structure desperately, knowing that it is your only hope as everything else around you drowns. This analogy demonstrates to us our state with Allah, aṣ-Ṣamad. He is the Eternal Refuge, the one whom we turn to because He never falters. This is example shows us how much we need Him when are in trouble, but in truth, He is aṣ-Ṣamad even when the sea is calm, and we are as in need of Him when things are fine as when they are not. This is because aṣ-Ṣamad is the One who controls the storm itself. Thus, aṣ-Ṣamad reminds us that He is the only permanent, reliable refuge we can turn to in all circumstances.

Aṣ-Ṣamad has many meanings, including the Eternal, the Master, and the One who is turned to.

▪ Al-Aḥad – Unique (112:1)

▪ When you are overwhelmed with difficulty.

▪ When things are going well in your life.

▪ Remind yourself that aṣ-Ṣamad is the only constant, the only One able to give you refuge in the storm.

Ya Ṣamad, You are always there for us when we are paralyzed by our fears, triggered by our anxiety and dispirited by our flaws. Help us overcome every storm.

Ponder upon times when you were up against a "storm", did you turn to and hold on to aṣ-Ṣamad?

القَادِر القَدِير المُقْتَدِر

AL-QĀDIR
AL-QADĪR
AL-MUQTADIR

THE POWERFUL, THE OMNIPOTENT, THE DETERMINER

'And to Allah belongs the dominion of the heavens and the earth,
and Allah is Powerful over everything.' (3:189)

STORY

Allah demonstrates to us His power throughout the Qur'an and in the physical world around us. The Qur'an tells us how Allah created Adam. It shows us how, in the story of the Prophet 'Uzayr, for example, Allah was able to bring back an entire village after it had been completely destroyed. It tells how seemingly powerful empires and tyrants were overpowered. Similarly, looking at the world around us reminds us of His power because He is the One who created this world, and the fact that even the most powerful person in the world is not perfect in his or her power reminds us that al-Qadīr is ultimately powerful, with no weakness or defect. Whatever difficulty we face, we have to thus remind ourselves that we can overcome it if we seek strength from Him. Indeed, when we recite the supplication of istikhāra, we say 'Astaqdiruka biqudratik… fa anta taqdir wa anā lā aqdir', which means 'I seek ability from You, by Your power… For indeed You have power, and I am powerless.' This formidable supplication reminds us that even when we face difficult or uncertain situations, we can overcome them by seeking strength with al-Qādir. When we fear someone overpowering us, we can remind ourselves that He is al-Muqtadir, and He has the perfect strength to aid us.

The One who is Omnipotent, has power over everything, and who has the power to decree and carry out His decree.

- Al-'Azīz – Almighty (54:42)
- Al-'Alīm – All-Knowing (42:50)

- When you feel weak, seek strength from the One who is Perfect in Power and Ability: Al-Qādir al-Qadīr al-Muqtadir.
- Remember that no matter how powerful a person appears to be, Allah is more powerful.
- Remember to use whatever power you have been given wisely.

Ya Qādir, You know what is good for us better than we do ourselves, Ya Qādir, decree the best for us and keep us protected from every evil.

When you feel unable, does knowing that Allah is the Omnipotent give you strength?

MEMORIZATION LIST

Ar-Raḥmān	1	O
Ar-Raḥīm	2	O
Al-Malik	3	O
Al-Quddūs	4	O
As-Salām	5	O
Al-Mu'min	6	O
Al-Muhaymin	7	O
Al-'Azīz	8	O
Al-Jabbār	9	O
Al-Mutakabbir	10	O
Al-Khāliq	11	O
Al-Bāri'	12	O
Al-Muṣawwir	13	O
Al-Ghaffār	14	O
Al-Qahhār	15	O
Al-Wahhāb	16	O
Ar-Razzāq	17	O
Al-Fattāḥ	18	O
Al-'Alīm	19	O
Al-Qābiḍ	20	O
Al-Bāsiṭ	21	O
Al-Khāfiḍ	22	O
Ar-Rāfi'	23	O
Al-Muizz	24	O
Al-Mudhill	25	O
As-Samī'	26	O
Al-Baṣīr	27	O
Al-Hakam	28	O
Al-'Adl	29	O
Al-Laṭīf	30	O
Al-Khabīr	31	O
Al-Ḥalīm	32	O
Al-'Aẓīm	33	O
Al-Ghafūr	34	O
Ash-Shakūr	35	O
Al-'Alī	36	O
Al-Kabīr	37	O
Al-Ḥafīẓ	38	O
Al-Muqīt	39	O
Al-Ḥasīb	40	O
Al-Jalīl	41	O
Al-Karīm	42	O
Ar-Raqīb	43	O
Al-Mujīb	44	O
Al-Wāsi'	45	O
Al-Ḥakīm	46	O
Al-Wadūd	47	O
Al-Majīd	48	O
Al-Bā'ith	49	O
Ash-Shahīd	50	O
Al-Haqq	51	O
Al-Wakīl	52	O
Al-Qawī	53	O
Al-Matīn	54	O
Al-Walī	55	O
Al-Ḥamīd	56	O
Al-Muḥsī	57	O
Al-Mubdi'	58	O
Al-Mu'īd	59	O
Al-Muḥyī	60	O
Al-Mumīt	61	O
Al-Ḥayy	62	O
Al-Qayyūm	63	O
Al-Wājid	64	O
Al-Mājid	65	O
Al-Wāḥid	66	O
Al-Aḥad	67	O
Aṣ-Ṣamad	68	O
Al-Qādir	69	O
Al-Qadīr	70	O
Al-Muqtadir	71	O
Al-Muqaddim	72	O
Al-Mu'akhir	73	O
Al-Awwal	74	O
Al-Ākhir	75	O
Az-Ẓāhir	76	O
Al-Bāṭin	77	O
Al-Walī	78	O
Al-Muta'āl	79	O
Al-Barr	80	O
At-Tawwāb	81	O
Al-Muntaqim	82	O
Al-'Afuww	83	O
Ar-Ra'ūf	84	O
Mālik al-Mulk	85	O
Dhū al-Jalāi wa al-Ikrām	86	O
Al-Muqsiṭ	87	O
Al-Jāmi'	88	O
Al-Ghanī	89	O
Al-Mughnī	90	O
Al-Māni'	91	O
Aḍ-Ḍārr	92	O
An-Nāfi'	93	O
An-Nūr	94	O
Al-Hādī	95	O
Al-Badī'	96	O
Al-Bāqī	97	O
Al-Wārith	98	O
Ar-Rashīd	99	O
Aṣ-Ṣabūr	100	O
Allāh	101	O

الْمُقَدِّم الْمُؤَخِّر

AL-MUQADDIM
AL-MU'AKHIR

THE ADVANCER, THE DELAYER

'You are the One Who brings forward and who delays, there is no deity worthy of worship but You.' (Muslim)

STORY

Sometimes we can be frustrated because we feel that we have been 'left behind'. Others have moved on with their lives and advanced, whether in their professional lives, their personal lives, or otherwise. There could be practical reasons, as Allah has placed us in a world of means, but if after significant effort on our part, we find that our perceived advancement is delayed, knowing that Allah is al-Muqaddim al-Mu'akhir helps us to know that what appear to be delays have a purpose, and we should be learning from where we are. Worldly advancement is not a reflection of one's station with Allah, but rather what we do with this advancement. Similarly, worldly delay is not an indication that Allah is displeased with us. In all cases, we should know that true advancement is spiritual advancement, and Allah advances those who work for His sake.

Al-Muqaddim al-Mu'akhir is the One who advances certain actions and delays others, and He also promotes some due to their good deeds while pushing others away due to their misdeeds.

- When you are frustrated at being behind.
- When you are impressed by someone's worldly advancement, remember that it is spiritual advancement that is important.
- When you become jealous of others' success.

Ya Muqaddim, Ya Mu'akhir, make us content with Your decree so that we do not like to hasten what You have delayed, nor delay what You have hastened.

What plans has Allah advanced for you and what plans has He delayed? Reflect on the significance and reason for that.

الأوَّل الآخِر

AL-AWWAL
AL-ĀKHIR

THE FIRST, THE LAST

'He is the First and the Last; the Outer and the Inner; He has knowledge of all things.' (57:3)

STORY

The things that are most important to us are those matters that preoccupy our thoughts and drive our actions. If we want to know what is the foremost issue on our mind, one that is a priority for us, it is usually the thing we first think of in the morning. It is also our ultimate aim. So, ask yourself: What is the first thing you think of when you wake up in the morning? And what is the last thing you think of at night? The fact that Allah is al-Awwal al-Ākhir tells us two important things: Since He is the First, He should be what we first consider when embarking upon anything and He should be the first in our hearts; and since He is the Last, and is the only One remaining after all is gone, our desires and intentions should be geared towards Him and His pleasure. This might be easier said than done. But if we take a moment to reflect, those things that are the 'first' for us as well as the 'last' in terms of what we intend, are temporary. What we give importance to is rooted in what we think is truly beneficial or gives us comfort. Yet, nothing is more beneficial than a relationship with Allah, and nothing can give more lasting comfort than that.

The One who is the First, and nothing was before Him, and the Last, so nothing will be after Him.

- Az-Ẓāhir, Al-Bāṭin – The Manifest, The Intimate (57:3)

- Wake up every morning expressing gratitude to Allah, and reciting the remembrances, to ensure that He is al-Awwal for you.
- Always reconsider what your end goal is, so that everything you do can be aimed towards al-Ākhir.

Ya Awwal, help us to think of you first before anything else, Ya Ākhir, enable us to direct all our intentions towards you as our ultimate aim.

Do you begin and end your day with the remembrance of Allah? Is Allah your first thought and last thought each day?

الظَّاهر الباطن

AŻ-ŻĀHIR
AL-BĀṬIN

THE MANIFEST, THE INTIMATE

'He is the First and the Last; the Outer and the Inner; He has knowledge of all things.' (57:3)

STORY

Throughout the Qur'an, Allah exhorts us to think, reflect, see, and ponder. He points out His signs; for example: 'Have they not seen that We conduct the water to a dry land, and with it We bring out vegetation from which their livestock eat, and they themselves? Do they not see?' (32:25) A sign by its very nature leads us somewhere, and our reflection on these signs should lead us to Allah. Indeed, He is aẓ-Ẓāhir, who manifests His signs in the universe - He becomes obvious through these signs. He is also al-Bāṭin, which means that, though He is manifest – ẓāhir – through His signs, we cannot conceive of Him fully. Worshipping Allah through these names should make us more conscious of both our external and internal – what we manifest and what is in our hearts. We should direct all our prayers to Him because no one is above Him, as well as crave a closeness to Him because no one knows us more intimately than Him. When we start worshipping Him by these names, we can start to see Allah's attributes as they manifest in the everyday and the ordinary, as well as in the awe-inspiring, and our hearts naturally want to come close to Him as we realize that He is with us always.

The One who manifests His lordship outwardly, yet is hidden with regards to sensory perception.

- Al-Awwal, Al-Ākhir – The First and The Last (2:54)

- When you feel far from Allah, ponder upon the manifestations of His signs in the universe.
- When you feel empty.
- Crave a connection with al-Bāṭin by purifying the parts of you that no one sees – your heart, your soul – and doing actions of His sake that only He knows of.

Ya Ẓāhir, Ya Bāṭin, there is nothing that is hidden from You and there is nothing that You don't know among that which is apparent. Help us identify and rectify our mistakes.

How often do you reflect on nature and the creation of the universe as a way of gaining closeness to Allah?

AL-BARR

THE MOST KIND, THE DOER OF GOOD

'Indeed, we used to call upon Him alone before. He is truly the Most Kind, Most Merciful.' **(52:28)**

STORY

Whenever we look around us, we can see the manifestations and traces of Allah's goodness and kindness. When He tells us that He is al-Barr, He is reminding us that His dealings with us are based on goodness. Thus, if we look at the world around us, even what seems to be bad, and remember that our Lord is al-Barr, we need to ask ourselves: what good could there be in this? And good is not simply what is outwardly good, but that causes good to come, in the form of encouraging us to be patient, or to stand up against injustice, or to do good to others. All tests are from al-Barr, meaning that their purpose is to raise our station - there is eventually good. Indeed, the verse cited refers to the people of Paradise, who remember when they used to call upon Allah, and affirm His kindness and mercy after what they see of the goodness that is given to them in Heaven. We should therefore also inculcate in us the characteristic of goodness, through purifying our hearts of anything negative towards others, and actively doing good for others, as the Qur'an exhorts us not simply to help others to do and be good while forgetting ourselves (2:44), and to encourage each other to do righteousness (58:9).

The One who is good, and delivers good to His servants.

- Ar-Raḥīm – The Especially Merciful
  (2:54)

- When you find yourself attached to what you have, give to others from what you love, as that is the way to attain virtue or goodness (birr – 3:92).
- When you find yourself being unkind to others.

Ya Barr, purify our hearts from hatred and envy for Muslims and replace them with virtue and goodness.

This name is paired with Ar-Raḥīm in the Qur'an; reflect on why that might be. Are you merciful and kind in your actions?

التَّوَّاب

AT-TAWWĀB

THE OFT-RELENTING, ACCEPTOR OF REPENTANCE

'Then highly exalt your Lord with praise and seek His forgiveness; indeed, He has always been Granting and Accepting of repentance.' (110:3)

STORY

All of us need to return to Allah. Some of us might feel far from Him in the sense that, while we do all our obligations, we are not conscious of Him in our daily lives. Others of us might be far from Him because we do the things He has prohibited. We might wonder if He will accept us, because we have been taught that there is no place for people like us. But He has named Himself at-Tawwāb to let us know that He will accept all those who return to Him sincerely, no matter where we have been or what we have done. Indeed, Allah was ready to accept Pharaoh, the worst tyrant to have ever lived, if he had repented to Him and made amends, so why would you think that there is no place for you? Indeed, Allah tells us in the Qur'an that He loves the tawwābīn – those who constantly return to Him. And who returns except the one who was far? Thus, it is on us to go back to Him, to do our utmost so stop the wrong that we do while doing good.

The One who accepts all those who turn back to Him.

- Ar-Raḥīm – The Especially Merciful (2:160)
- Al-Ḥakīm – Most Wise (24:10)

- When you have committed a sin.
- When you feel far from Him.
- When you have sinned so much you feel you are at the point of no return.

Ya Tawwāb, accept our turning back to You and forgive us for our sins.

Did you used to refrain from turning back to Allah because you were afraid that you would not be able to stop a certain sin? Does knowing that At-Tawwāb accepts those who return help you in taking that step towards Him?

AL-MÚNTAQIM

THE AVENGER

'And on the Day We seize [them] mightily We shall exact retribution.' (44:16)

STORY

Many people grew up on superhero stories and have their favorites. These superheroes fight on the side of the downtrodden, the forgotten, and the marginalized. When a system only works for the powerful, the superhero steps in to protect and avenge the wronged. Part of the reason for their appeal is that we have been created with a desire for justice; however, when justice is not served, it can cause even more wrongdoing through acts of vengeance that go beyond the requirements of justice. Thus, Allah reminds us that He has taken it upon Himself to avenge the wronged and that He will do so with true justice, because He is al-'Adl as well. This should remind us that when we are wronged, it does not justify going beyond the bounds. It should also remind us of the importance of establishing justice on earth, in order to avoid Allah's punishment over unjust systems. Finally, we should be wary of transgressing against others, as Allah will take their right from us, either in this life or the next.

He is the One who avenges the wronged and punishes the wrongdoers.

SITUATION
- When you are feeling vengeful, do not seek vengeance for yourself but, rather, know that Allah will avenge for all those who are wronged.
- When you feel despair that it appears that wrongdoers have gotten away with their evil, remember al-Muntaqim will deal with them at the best time.

DU'A

Ya Muntaqim, allow us to repent from any injustice we have committed so that we can avoid Your punishment.

REFLECTIVE QUESTION
Do you seek vengeance rather than justice? Does this sometimes make you overstep the limits?

AL-'AFUWW

THE PARDONER

'For those—hopefully Allah will pardon them, for Allah has always been Pardoning, Oft-Forgiving.' (4:99)

STORY

When we make mistakes in our relationships with human beings, the greater our transgression, or the more frequent, the more irreparable the relationship is. Indeed, sometimes small mistakes are brought up again in arguments, showing that the person has not truly forgotten or forgiven – perhaps we have even been that person. Some relationships can never go back to how they were after a rupture or break in trust. Because this is our experience with other people, we somehow think that this is our relationship with Allah too. But Allah is far above – He is al-'Afuww. This means that whatever mistakes we made – no matter how grand – He can not only forgive them (and He forgives completely – He is al-Ghafūr) but delete them entirely from our records. Imagine being on the Day of Judgment, expecting to be held accountable for something you did, only to find that there is no mention of it in your records. Allah can grant you that blank slate again and enable you to reset your relationship with Him in this life. Remember that Allah pardons those transgressions against Himself, but what you do against people, you should try to amend with them.

Allah is the One who pardons completely, such that the sin is completely erased, with no traces.

- Al-Ghafūr – Oft-Forgiving (22:60)
- Al-Qadīr – All-Powerful (4:149)

- When you feel that your past sins are still holding you back.
- Ask for afū (pardon), particularly during the last ten nights of Ramadan, as our Beloved ﷺ advised his wife Aisha to do so.
- Pardon people who have wronged you in order that Allah pardons you.

O Allah, You are 'Afuww, You love to pardon, so pardon us.

Have you felt that some mistakes you made were unforgivable? How do you feel now knowing that Allah can completely reset your records?

الرَّؤُوف

AR-RA'ŪF

THE COMPASSIONATE, THE ALL-PITYING

'And of mankind is one who sells his (inner)self, seeking Allah's pleasure. And Allah is Compassionate towards the servants.' (2:207)

STORY

Imagine for a second that an extremely sick child must take a bitter but life-saving medicine, and there is no alternative. This child screams and resists taking the medicine, crying so much that anyone's heart would break. The parents, however, hold the child down and force him to take the medicine. While the outward actions are not gentle and appear to have no compassion in them, everyone knows that at the essence of the parents' actions is love and mercy. This would be described as raḥma. As the child cries, the parents hug and hold their child, telling him or her words of love and encouragement, explaining why they had to give him the medicine. This is overflowing mercy – ra'fa. Raḥma may be used for what internally or externally has mercy, but ra'fa is only what is overtly and intensely merciful. Thus Allah tells us that He is also ra'ūf with us, meaning that many times in our lives we will see intense, beautiful, and overt manifestations of mercy and compassion in our lives. It could be through someone comforting us when we are down, or someone helping us when we need it the most. These are all manifestations of His ra'fa.

MEANING

He is the One who exhibits intense mercy and pity towards His servants.

SITUATION

- When someone does something kind for you.
- Reflect upon all the times you felt Allah's intense mercy towards you.

DU'A

Ya Ra'ūf, bestow upon us Your mercy and enable us to recognize it, so that we may be grateful.

PAIRING

- Ar-Raḥīm – Especially Merciful (57:9)

REFLECTIVE QUESTION

When was the last time you felt Allah's mercy in your life? Do you show mercy to others?

المُقْسِط

AL-MUQSIṬ

THE EQUITABLE

'Allah is a Witness that there is no god except Him—and so are the angels and people of knowledge. He is the Maintainer of justice (qist). There is no god except Him—the Almighty, All-Wise.' (3:18)

STORY

We might often wonder how we will be judged. We wonder if our circumstances will be taken to account. We wonder if we will be held against the standard of the memorizer of Qur'an, or of the generous wealthy person, or of the scholar. Knowing Allah is al-Muqsiṭ means that He is the Most Equitable and Just, and will judge us according to the standards that He has set while taking into account our circumstances. For example, we will not be judged by the quantity of what we gave, but by our generosity in relation to what we have and our intention while giving. This means that a generous poor person who donates his only meal to someone more needy than him for the sole purpose of pleasing Allah will be given the same (or more) reward as the generous wealthy person who donates much of his wealth to charity for the same reason. Therefore, we have to be confident in al-Muqsiṭ, and know that we will all be judged, at the very least, fairly, but we always hope in His mercy over His justice. Finally, Allah being al-Muqsiṭ does not mean that we can blame circumstances when we have been given the ability to change them. No one will be tested more than they can bear and whatever Allah asks of us, it is because He knows that we are able to undertake it.

He is the One who is most equitable, balanced and just.

- When we see others doing more and worshipping more yet we feel restricted in our ability and circumstances to do so.
- Allah orders us in multiple places in the Qur'an to be fair and just. We should cultivate this trait, as well as take people's circumstances into account.

Ya Muqsiṭ, help us to be fair and equitable with others, even if it were against our own selves.

Do you take into account people's circumstances when you interact with them?

AL-JĀMI'

THE GATHERER

'Allah—there is no god except He. He will surely gather you to the Day of Resurrection about which there is no doubt. And who is truer in discourse than Allah?' (4:87)

STORY

In this life, we might be joined to different people based on our circumstances or affiliations. We might be far from certain people and closer to others. It is easy to forget that we will all – every single human being from the beginning of time until the end of time – be gathered together on the Day of Judgment. Al-Jāmi' is the One who brings us together and, on that day, our skin color, our nationality, our wealth, our political party – none of that will matter. We will be gathered together to be judged before the Most High, and everyone will be judged individually. However, we are also told in the Qur'an that 'those who disbelieved will be driven to Hell in groups' (39:71) and 'those who feared their Lord will be driven to Paradise in groups' (39:73). Al-Jāmi' will thus gather us with those whom we are most like spiritually, and it is those people whom we will dwell eternally with. Thus we need to always look at our surroundings and company and ask: is this a group I would like to be gathered with on the Day of Judgment? Of course, we refrain from passing judgment on people's spiritual states, but we should ensure that wherever we are, we are encouraged to do and be good, rather than the opposite.

Allah is the Gatherer who brings together different elements in this life, and will gather everyone together on the Day of Judgement.

- When you are in a questionable environment.
- When you feel alone, ask Al-Jāmi' to gather you with others who are righteous in this life and the next.
- Whoever you find yourself with, ask: is this with whom I want to be gathered with on the Day of Judgement?

Ya Jāmi', gather us on the Day of Judgement with the prophets, the righteous, and those who have earned Your pleasure.

Reflect on the people in your life, whom would you like to be gathered with in Jannah?

الْغَنِي الْمُغْنِي

AL-GHANĪ
AL-MUGHNĪ

THE SELF-SUFFICIENT, THE ENRICHER

'Thus your Lord is the Self-Sufficient, the Possessor of mercy.'
(6:133)

STORY

Everyone that we can ever turn to is limited. Indeed, we ourselves are limited. We might be restricted by circumstance, by resources, or by ability. These limitations are part of being human, and they exist because we have needs. Thus, anyone whom we ask for help will always be restricted by certain factors and by their own needs. Not al-Ghanī – He is the Self-Sufficient, the Rich. We turn to Him for all our needs because we understand that He is not limited by anything; indeed, He can create limits for others, but He Himself is limitless. Moreover, this should impact the way that we worship because we realize that He does not need our prayers; rather, we need to pray to and worship Him. We do not benefit al-Ghanī by anything that we do, nor do we harm Him by anything we do or fail to do, but we are ultimately benefited if He accepts our actions from us or if He chooses to forgive us. And He is not simply Self-Sufficient, but He is al-Mughnī. He enriches His righteous servants through granting them spiritual wealth, strength, and sufficiency from others.

Al-Ghanī is the Self-Sufficient, who has no needs, and al-Mughnī is the One who enriches others.

- Al-Ḥamīd - Praiseworthy (57:24)
- Al-Karīm - The Generous (27:40)

SITUATION

- When people let us down, we should be understanding because we recognize that people — even those who love us the most — are limited and have their own needs. Only Allah is Self-Sufficient.
- We should worship Allah knowing that He does not benefit from our worship nor is He harmed by our lack of worship; rather we need to acknowledge that we need to worship Him.

DU'A

Ya Ghanī, Ya Mughnī, fulfill our needs for us and grant us sufficiency through You.

REFLECTIVE QUESTION

If you have ever felt frustrated because people have not been there for you in the way that you wanted or envisioned, how does knowing that Allah is al-Ghanī help you to understand their limitations?

AL-MĀNI'

THE PREVENTER

'There is no withholder of what you have given, and no giver to what You have withheld.' (Bukhari & Muslim)

STORY

Allah creates means for our protection. He has created the Qur'an and the example of the Prophet ﷺ and the righteous in order that spiritual harm is prevented. He has ordered us to utilize physical means to prevent harm from ourselves as well as from others. And part of worshipping Allah by this name is by utilizing these means. The other meaning of this name is that He Himself withholds at times — but He only withholds from people due to His mercy and wisdom. When we feel that we have been prevented from something, we should always seek the wisdom behind it and understand that there is a purpose. Perhaps you have been withheld from a job you really wanted, a spouse you wanted to marry, a country you wanted to live in. This does not mean that we are not supposed to work hard to achieve our goals — indeed, the Prophet ﷺ was 'prevented' from Ta'if because Allah knew that it was not the best for him — but he still worked to obtain protection from other tribes. He was eventually granted Madina.

Al-Mani' is the One who creates the causes to prevent both physical and spiritual harm, and He withholds from people in order to benefit them.

- When you feel like you have been prevented from something that you wanted.
- Be a preventer of harm, but do not ever prevent good from reaching others.
- When you know that only Allah has the power to prevent and withhold, ask Him from His bounty, and use the means of protections that He has given to prevent harm from yourself, especially spiritual harm.

Ya Māni', there is no withholder of what you have given, and no giver to what You have withheld, so grant us from Your bounty and protect us from harm.

Reflect on the times that you have been prevented from something, but it ended up being good for you.

الضَّار النَّافع

AḌ-ḌĀRR
AN-NĀFI'

THE ONE WHO HARMS, THE ONE WHO BENEFITS

'Do you worship, apart from Allah, what can neither benefit you in anything nor harm you?' (21:66)

STORY

A story was narrated about a woman who fell down and cut herself. Instead of cursing or even crying, she laughed. A man who saw her was incredulous, 'What is wrong with you? You fall down and laugh?' She responded, 'At first, I was focused on the pain, but when I realized that anything that harms a believer is a cause for forgiveness, and if I am patient Allah has promised a reward without reckoning, I was overjoyed! This is why I laughed.' This woman knew Allah is aḍ-Ḍārr an-Nāfi', she was seeing beyond what appeared to be harmful and saw the benefit in it. Outwardly, it was bad - she was hurt after all - but she realized the blessings in it. Instead of focusing on the harm itself, she focused on the only One who can truly harm and benefit. Indeed, when the magicians at the time of Pharaoh were threatened with crucifiction, they said to him, 'so decree whatever you decree; you can only decree for this Earlier Life.' (20:72) While it appeared that Pharaoh had the power to harm, He was ultimately drowned and will be sent to hell, while the magicians were ultimately benefited by their conviction and will be rewarded with Paradise. Indeed, Paradise is the ultimate benefit, while Hell is the ultimate harm. We should thus know that what is truly harmful is what Allah has said is harmful – lying, cheating, abusing, and worshipping other than Him – and what is truly beneficial is what He has informed us of – praying with devotion, being good to others, and preferring the Hereafter.

Benefit and harm are ultimately from Allah, but what is harmful on the surface has benefit in it.

- Whenever you are faced with harm, ask yourself what you can learn from it, and turn to Allah sincerely to remove it.
- When you are tempted to do something which goes against what is halal but it gives you a worldly benefit.

Ya Ḍārr Ya Nāfi', only You have the power to harm and to benefit, so remove from us all worldly and otherworldly harm, and bring us benefit in both this life and the next.

What might be a spiritual benefit to an outwardly hardship you had to endure?

النُّور

A N - N Ū R

THE LIGHT

'Allah is the Light of the heavens and the earth.' (24:35)

STORY

The basic characteristic of light is that it illuminates. What was in darkness becomes visible and what was hidden becomes manifest. The effects of this light is manifold: we can gain understanding, find the right path, and gain clarity. Light is something that we know intrinsically is good, and it makes us feel that the world around us is expansive. Indeed, we sometimes describe an uplifting or pious person as having light. While we do not know the true nature of the light of an-Nūr, what we do know is that by His light darkness is dispelled: whether that is darkness we feel in our souls or other than that. We know that He guides us by illuminating the way for us, and indeed the Qur'an is called a 'light' because it does precisely that. In the Chapter of An-Nūr in the Qur'an, Allah tells us that 'Allah is the Light of the heavens and the earth. The parable of His light is as a niche wherein is a lamp; the lamp is in a glass; the glass is like a glittering planet, kindled from a blessed tree—an olive tree—neither eastern nor western. Its oil would almost illuminate even if no fire were to touch it. Light upon light. Allah guides to His light whomever He wills. Thus Allah sets forth parables for mankind. For Allah is All-Knowing of everything.' (24:35) Some of the exegetes of the Qur'an state that this is an analogy to the heart of a believer that is touched with the light of an-Nūr and is thus illuminated. When your heart is illuminated, you can then bring light into this world and into the lives of others.

An-Nūr is the Light, and the Source of light, and He illuminates everything in darkness.

- Whenever you feel that you are in a dark place, ask Allah to put light in your soul and to show you the way.
- When you feel lost, the best way to access Allah's light is through the Qur'an and the example of His Prophet ﷺ.

Ya Nūr, make for me light, and illuminate the way to You.

How can you become a source of 'light' for others?

الهَادِي

AL-HĀDT

THE GUIDE

'But sufficient is your Lord as a Guide and Supporter.' (25:31)

STORY

When we want to reach a destination, we usually rely on a guide. We might use google maps or ask someone who knows where we want to get to to show us the way. We ask our guides not only to show us a way, but the best way. And if we get lost or veer off path due to distraction, we return to our guides to get us back on track. However, when we are not cognizant of our destination, we can be distracted by the many different roads and streets, and may be tempted to follow dangerous roads to unsavory destinations. We might even follow those who lead us off the path we are supposed to be on. When Allah is telling us that He is al-Hādī – the Guide – He is telling us that He can show us the best way to our ultimate destination: Paradise and His pleasure. If that is where we want to go, He will guide us to the straight, most uncomplicated path to it. The fact that He named Himself al-Hādī is to let you know that you can ask Him for His guidance at any time, and He has taken it upon Himself to show you the way. When we feel lost or confused, we need to know that we can always turn to al-Hādī. Part of His guidance is sending the Qur'an and His Prophet ﷺ to lead us to Him. Now ponder upon this: al-Hādī is not simply the Guide, but our destination as well - and who better to get us to Him than Him?

MEANING

Allah is the One who guides all creation to what benefits them in this life and the next.

SITUATION

- Whenever you feel confusion, ask al-Hādī to guide you.
- When you feel that you are on the wrong path, turn to al-Hādī.
- Al-Hādī not only guides, but He places signs to lead you to Him; thus, we should look at what He has created as guidance.

PAIRING

- An-Naṣīr - The Supporter (25:31)

DU'A

Ya Hādī, guide us in our goals so that we may carry them out in accordance with what You expect from us.

REFLECTIVE QUESTION

Reflect on your goals in life, have you called upon al-Hādī enough to guide you to them? When you feel confused in your faith, do you call upon Him to guide you to the right way?

AL-BADI'

'Originator of the heavens and the earth—how can He have offspring when He never had a consort? And He created every-thing, and He is All-Knowing of everything.' (6:101)

STORY

Human beings are impressed by originality. When, for example, a new phone comes out that 'changes the game', so to speak, we marvel at the design. We are impressed by the ease of use and the ability to make our lives easier. We want to invest in the most innovative companies, and look up to the creative mavens who are able to think outside the box. In truth, as impressive as these inventions are, they build upon what came before. Yet Allah is al-Badi' – the Originator. Do we ever look at the creation of the heavens and the earth in such a way that we are struck by their sheer originality and extraordinary nature? Allah has provided for us the building blocks to make new things, but we cannot actually go outside of or beyond them. Yet if we look at the creation of al-Badi' – the sheer number and variation of fruits and vegetables, animals and plants, our own selves – we can come close to understanding what true originality and invention mean.

MEANING

Al-Badi' is the one who creates that which has no precedent; His creation is completely original and innovative.

SITUATION

- When we come across an invention or novelty, it should always bring us back to al-Badi' and remind us of what true originality is.
- When we reflect on the creations of the heavens and the earth as a way to come close to Allah by His name al-Badi'.

DU'A

Ya Badi', help us to remember You when we witness what You have created.

REFLECTIVE QUESTION

Reflect on your day- to-day life and write down a list of all of the things that Allah has originated.

الْبَاقِي

AL-BĀQĪ

THE EVERLASTING

*'And there will remain the Face of your Lord, Owner of
Majesty and Honor.'* (55:27)

STORY

Everything in this world has an ending – whether it is the good times or the bad, life itself, relationships, and so much more. This is the nature of the world. Al-Bāqī reminds us that everything ends – except Him. Everyone leaves - He remains. So what is the point of attaching ourselves to what is temporary, rather than directing our efforts and attaching ourselves to the One who lasts? If we work for this world, we may obtain everything we want therein, but the pleasure will be temporary. Yet the work done for Allah – doing the deeds that He loves, investing in our relationship with and connection to Him – remains because He remains. The Qur'an is replete with stories of those who were oppressed but stood firm because they knew that whatever hardship they were undergoing would end, but '… what Allah has is lasting. And We will surely give those who were patient their reward according to the best of what they used to do.' (16:96) This does not mean that we should not enjoy the parts of life that Allah has put enjoyment in - family, friends, and wonderful experiences - but that we should not be deceived into thinking that they will always be there.

Al-Bāqī is the One who has no end, and remains after everything else is gone.

- Whenever something of this world ends and we feel a little heartbroken, we should remind ourselves that we should hold on to Allah, because He is al-Bāqī.
- Knowing that Allah is al-Bāqī should encourage us to invest in the things that will last and are pleasing to Him, and the things that will benefit us after we have passed.

Ya Bāqī, allow us to hold on to You for You are everlasting.

Have you ever relied upon someone or something so much but then it didn't last? How did that make you feel and how could you remember al-Bāqī during these times?

الوَارِث

AL-WĀRITH

THE INHERITOR

'And indeed, it is We who give life and cause death, and We are the Inheritor.' (15:23)

STORY

Whenever we think of inheritance, we think of what we will be leaving behind for our families and loved ones. Al-Wārith reminds us to think more expansively than that: 'What are we leaving behind for our Hereafter? What good are we leaving that will benefit us and others after we pass?' This is the true inheritance that we leave behind that will cause us, as the Qur'an tells us, to inherit Paradise. Moreover, knowing that we will be separated from everything that we ever owned and that it will pass on to other possessors should change our relationship with our possessions. We should view them as a trust that we will be asked about and that they will eventually return to the true possessor – al-Wārith, the One who 'inherits'' everything and to whom everything will return. Furthermore, the best inheritance we can leave, especially as parents, is a righteous upbringing for our children and leading by example. In numerous places in the Qur'an, Allah reminds us that the children of righteous parents were protected because of the goodness of their parents.

Al-Wārith is the One to whom everything will return.

- Always think about what you will be leaving behind, and work to leave behind the best works.
- Break your attachment to worldly possessions by reminding yourself that you will eventually be separated from them, and all will return to al-Wārith.

Ya Wārith everything I have will eventually return to You, please do not let me despair when it leaves my possession.

What legacy are you leaving behind? What good works are you leaving that will, inshAllah, make a lasting impact?

الرَّشيد

AR-RÁSHĪD

THE RIGHT IN GUIDANCE

'The right course (al-rushd) has become clear from the wrong.' (2:256)

STORY

When you want to ask for advice from someone about what path to take, you will – if you are intelligent and sincere – go to someone who is wise. This way, you can trust that their advice will be beneficial and that, if you follow it, you will not only get to the destination you want to, but you will learn much along the way. Ar-Rashīd directs and guides us along the path in order that we might reach Paradise. When we trust that Allah guides and directs with His wisdom, we should know that whatever path we are taken upon, there is wisdom and we will learn something from it. This is even when the road itself seems dark, or we went through a scary experience. Since we are with ar-Rashīd, we trust that there is something to be learned. Indeed, if one has an expert coach that they trust, even when the coach puts them through a gruelling exercise or makes them do something that doesn't seem to make sense, they go through it because they know that the coach knows what it is best. Ar-Rashīd directs us to Paradise, and every obstacle or difficulty that comes in the way actually brings us closer to it, rather than farther away.

MEANING

Ar-Rashīd is the One who guides and directs His servants through His wisdom.

SITUATION

- Make the best of whatever situation you are in, knowing that it is from ar-Rashīd.
- Be a guide for people to the right path, and base the guidance on wisdom.

DU'A

Ya Rashīd, guide us through every step of our life.

REFLECTIVE QUESTION

Think of a time when Allah guided you in a very unique way. What did it teach you about ar-Rashīd?

Allah is the Light, the Guide, and He guides through Wisdom; how does that comfort you?

الصّبور

AṢ-ṢABŪR

THE PATIENT

'And if Allah were to impose blame on the people for what they have earned, He would not leave upon the earth any creature. But He defers them for a specified term. And when their time comes, then indeed Allah has ever been, of His servants, Seeing.' (35:45)

STORY

Many of us give up on ourselves before even starting. In the spiritual realm, we look at those who are pious and think that we could never be like them. Some religious obligations feel hard for us, even though they seem so easy for others! We may think that we are so behind everyone else. Does this mean we are doomed? Does it mean that Allah does not love us? Does it mean he has rejected us? On the contrary, Allah aṣ-Ṣabūr tells us that He is patient; He does not expect you to get everything right all of the time. He knows that at times, you take two steps forward and one step back, or even one step forward and two steps back. But what aṣ-Ṣabūr is telling us is because He is patient with us, we too should be patient with ourselves, especially when we are sincerely trying. Aṣ-Ṣabūr sees and witnesses all, but He still gives all of us the chance to become better. This, of course, does not mean that we do not try anymore because we know He is aṣ-Ṣabūr, but rather we know we can take baby steps to Him, and He comes to us at speed.

Aṣ-Ṣabūr is the One who shows patience with His servants, giving them the opportunity to return to Him and to become better.

- When you are frustrated with yourself for messing up remember that Allah appreciates your efforts and is patient with you so that you can return.

Ya Ṣabūr, grant us patience in every matter.

How can you cultivate a practice of patience in your life, being patient with yourself but also being patient with others? If Allah is patient with us, why can't we be patient with others?

ALLĀH

*'But as for me, He is Allah, my Lord, and I never associate
anyone with my Lord.'* (18:38)

STORY

Allāh is His unique name. When we call upon Allāh, we are calling upon Him by all the names and attributes discussed in this planner, and more. We call upon Him knowing that He is the only One who can answer, knowing that He treats us with His divine love and mercy, and knowing that He hears our every thought and prayer. We understand by this name that we cannot and should not turn to anything else in worship, even the subtle enticements of this world. It is this name that should inspire awe in us and love for our creator — for Allāh.

Allāh is the worshipped One, the only One worthy of worship, who has the best, most excellent, and most beautiful names and attributes.

Whenever we recite any of the remembrances, we remind ourselves of Allāh. This name should cause calm in our hearts as we know that He is with us always.

Ya Allāh, enable us to understand Your Names and incorporate them in our lives.

After reflecting on the names in this planner, does the name Allah inspire you to think from a different perspective about who Allah is?

SOURCES

Al-Ashqar, Umar Sulayman. *Sharḥ Ibn Al-Qayyim Li Asmā' Allāh Al-Ḥusnā*. Amman: Dar al-Nafā'is, 2008

Al-Ghazali, Abu Hamid. *The Ninety-Nine Beautiful Names of God: Al-Maqṣad Al-Asnā Fi Sharḥ Asmā' Allāh Al-Ḥusnā*. Translated by David Burrell and Nazih Daher. The Ghazālī Series. Cambridge: The Islamic Texts Society, 1992.

Hanuf, Safwan Mahmoud. *Al-Ism Al-Rabbānī Wa Atharuhu Fī as-Sulūk Al-Insānī*. 1st ed. Beirut: Dār al-Ma'rifa, 2004

Ibn Ajība, Aḥmad. *Allah: An Explanation of the Divine Names and Attributes*. Translated by Abdelaziz Suraqah. USA: Al-Madina Institute, 2014.

Muqaddim, Maher. *Asmā' Allāh Al-Ḥusnā: Jalālahā Wa Laṭāif Iqtirānihā Wa Thamarātihā Fī Ḍaw' Al-Kitāb Wal-Sunnah*. 3rd Ed. Kuwait: Al-Imam al-Thahabi, 2014.

Yaqeen Institute, Names of series, available online at https://yaqeeninstitute.org/series/names-of-allah (various authors)

Yousef, Jinan. *Reflecting on the Names of Allah,* London: Al-Buruj Press, 2020

9 798330 550807